THE MANHATTAN PROJECT

THE MANHATTAN PROJECT

THE MAKING OF THE ATOMIC BOMB

AL CIMINO

ARCTURUS

Picture credits

Corbis: 37, 48 (Hulton-Deutsch Collection), 60, 73, 74, 76, 88, 168 (SuperStock), 169 (Bettmann), 175, 187.

ARCTURUS

This edition published in 2016 by Arcturus Publishing Limited
26/27 Bickels Yard, 151–153 Bermondsey Street,
London SE1 3HA

ISBN: 978-1-78599-021-2
DA004652UK

Printed in China

Contents

Introduction

In 1913, H. G. Wells wrote a book called *The World Set Free* in which he envisaged an atomic bomb. He got many of the details wrong. However, his bombs were made from 'lumps of pure Carolinum', a fictional radioactive element – transuranic elements, such as the plutonium used in the first atomic explosion in 1945, had yet to be discovered. And Wells says 'A man could carry about in a handbag an amount of latent energy sufficient to wreck half a city'.

His bombs '. . . made a mighty thunder in the air, and fell like Lucifer'. They produced '. . . tremendous pillars of fire . . . Hard upon the sound of them came a roaring wind, and the sky was filled with flickering lightnings and rushing clouds.' They destroyed buildings like a scythe cutting down grass, while mountainous clouds billowed up into the air.

The book was published in 1914, just as World War I was starting. In 1932, the Hungarian physicist Leo Szilard, a Wells fan, read the book. The following year, he realized that you could indeed make an atomic bomb. He went on to patent the invention and, fearful that Nazi Germany might build such a device, alerted the British and American authorities to its possibilities.

He then went to work with other émigré physicists to make

The English author, futurist and socialist H. G. Wells (1866-1946), who envisaged the invention and use of atomic bombs in one of his novels.

a nuclear weapon and was a mainstay, if a troublesome one, of the Manhattan Project, the American-led programme to build a bomb. So Szilard could claim to be the father of the atomic bomb. Or was it Wells? In the first memorandum passed to President Roosevelt, outlining the possibility of making a bomb, Szilard's first citation is to *The World Set Free*.

In the book, Wells's atomic bombs were used in a war that pits an alliance of Britain, France and, perhaps, America against Germany and Austria. The war takes place in 1956. As a result, all the major cities of the world are destroyed. A conference is then called in Switzerland where Britain's 'King Egbert' abdicates in favour of a world state. Limitless atomic energy then solves the world's problems, leaving the majority of the world's population to pursue a career as artists.

Wells died in August 1946, a year after the atomic bomb had been used for the first time and ten months after the United Nations had been established, so he may have felt justified in his optimism. Many of the scientists who worked on the Manhattan Project did not.

However, what they had done has no equal in history. In a few short years, they had taken an arcane piece of theoretical physics and, with a massive investment of money, materiel and manpower, had turned it into a weapon of immense power, the like of which had never been seen. Along the way they had created entirely new technologies and, in secret, a vast industry that sprawled across America. Despite this titanic effort, until the test of the first bomb on 16 July 1945, many of them did not believe that it was going to go off.

Almost as amazing, for me at least, is that the place where Leo Szilard had his eureka moment and realized that it was possible to make an atomic bomb is just around the corner from my flat in Bloomsbury where I am writing this.

Al Cimino, London, February 2015

Chapter One
The Einstein Letter

On 2 August 1939, Albert Einstein, the world's most famous scientist – the Nobel laureate who had stood the world of physics on its head with his theories of relativity – sent a letter to the President of the United States, Franklin Delano Roosevelt. It said:

Sir:

Some recent work by E. Fermi and L. Szilard, which has been communicated to me in manuscript, leads me to expect that the element uranium may be turned into a new and important source of energy in the immediate future. Certain aspects of the situation which has arisen seem to call for watchfulness and if necessary, quick action on the part of the Administration. I believe therefore that it is my duty to bring to your attention the following facts and recommendations.

In the course of the last four months it has been made probable through the work of Joliot in France as well as Fermi and Szilard in America that it may be possible to set up a nuclear chain reaction in a large mass of uranium, by which vast amounts of power and large quantities of new radium-like elements would be generated. Now it appears almost certain that this could be achieved in the immediate future.

This new phenomenon would also lead to the construction of bombs, and it is conceivable – though much less certain – that extremely powerful bombs of this type may thus be constructed. A single bomb of this type, carried by boat and exploded in a port, might very well destroy the whole port together with some of the surrounding territory. However, such bombs might very well prove too heavy for transportation by air.

The United States has only very poor ores of uranium in moderate quantities. There is some good ore in Canada and former Czechoslovakia, while the most important source of uranium is in the Belgian Congo.

In view of this situation you may think it desirable to have some permanent contact maintained between the Administration and the group of physicists working on chain reactions in America. One possible way of achieving this might be for you to entrust the task with a person who has your confidence and who could perhaps serve in an unofficial capacity. His task might comprise the following:

a) to approach Government Departments, keep them informed of the further development, and put forward recommendations for Government action, giving particular attention to the problem of securing a supply of uranium ore for the United States.

b) to speed up the experimental work, which is at present being carried on within the limits of the budgets of university laboratories, by providing funds, if such funds be required, through his contacts with private persons who are willing to make contributions for this cause, and perhaps also by obtaining co-operation of industrial laboratories which have necessary equipment.

I understand that Germany has actually stopped the sale of uranium from the Czechoslovakian mines which she has taken over. That she should have taken such early action might perhaps be understood on the ground that the son of the German Under-Secretary of State, von Weizsacker, is attached to the Kaiser Wilhelm Institute in Berlin, where some of the American work on uranium is now being repeated.

Yours very truly,
Albert Einstein

The letter was to be delivered by Alexander Sachs, a Wall Street economist and unofficial advisor to the president, along with a memorandum prepared by Hungarian émigré physicist Leo Szilard, the man who had first conceived of the possibility of making an atomic bomb six years earlier and the author of the letter Einstein had signed.

Although he was a longtime friend, even Sachs had trouble getting in to see Roosevelt, who was busy dealing with the situation in Europe. On 23 August 1939, Nazi Germany and the Soviet Union signed a non-aggression pact. European armies began to mobilize and on 1 September Hitler invaded Poland, precipitating World War II.

It was not until 11 October that Sachs got in to see the president. Sachs had read Einstein's letter and Szilard's memorandum, and explained that recent research on chain reactions utilizing uranium made it probable that large amounts of power could be produced – enough to make extremely powerful bombs. The German government was actively supporting research in this area and it would be sensible if the US government did the same. Initially, Roosevelt was noncommittal and worried about finding the money for such research, but at a second meeting over breakfast the next morning he became convinced of the value of exploring atomic energy.

Leo Szilard was one of a number of European scientists who had fled to the United States in the 1930s to escape the Nazis. He and fellow Hungarian refugees Edward Teller and Eugene Wigner regarded it as their duty to alert Americans to the possibility that German scientists might win the race to build an atomic bomb. If they did, it was clear that Hitler would be more than willing to use such a weapon.

Roosevelt wrote back to Einstein on 19 October 1939, telling him that he had set up a committee consisting of Sachs and representatives from the Army and Navy to study the use of uranium. He believed that the US could not take the risk of allowing Hitler to achieve unilateral possession of an atomic bomb.

Szilard, Teller, Wigner and Italian physicist Enrico Fermi would all be involved in the project. The British were also working on building an atomic bomb, but they did not have the resources to pursue a fully fledged research programme while fighting for their survival. Nor were their facilities safe from airborne attack. Consequently, the British acceded, albeit reluctantly, to US leadership and sent their scientists to the States.

Despite Allied fears, the Germans put their scientific energies into areas such as jet fighters and rockets – the V1 and V2. By the end of the war, they would be scarcely nearer to producing atomic weapons than they had been at the beginning. However, the Americans and the émigré scientists were not to know that.

Elsewhere, work in France under Frédéric Joliot at the Radium Institute in Paris was halted during the German occupation. Joliot had smuggled his notes and materials to England, and joined the Resistance.

The Russian atomic research programme grew increasingly active as the war drew on. But, again, there were other priorities and the first successful Soviet test was not conducted until 1949. The Japanese managed to build several cyclotrons

Albert Einstein
Old Grove Rd.
Nassau Point
Peconic, Long Island

August 2nd, 1939

F.D. Roosevelt,
President of the United States,
White House
Washington, D.C.

Sir:

Some recent work by E.Fermi and L. Szilard, which has been communicated to me in manuscript, leads me to expect that the element uranium may be turned into a new and important source of energy in the immediate future. Certain aspects of the situation which has arisen seem to call for watchfulness and, if necessary, quick action on the part of the Administration. I believe therefore that it is my duty to bring to your attention the following facts and recommendations:

In the course of the last four months it has been made probable - through the work of Joliot in France as well as Fermi and Szilard in America - that it may become possible to set up a nuclear chain reaction in a large mass of uranium,by which vast amounts of power and large quantities of new radium-like elements would be generated. Now it appears almost certain that this could be achieved in the immediate future.

This new phenomenon would also lead to the construction of bombs, and it is conceivable - though much less certain - that extremely powerful bombs of a new type may thus be constructed. A single bomb of this type, carried by boat and exploded in a port, might very well destroy the whole port together with some of the surrounding territory. However, such bombs might very well prove to be too heavy for transportation by air.

a64a01

The first page of Albert Einstein's original letter of 2 August 1939 to President Roosevelt about the use of uranium to produce a nuclear bomb and potential sources of the ore.

by the war's end. These were key in the development of the atomic bomb, but the research effort could not be maintained in the face of increasing scarcities.

Only the US, as a late entrant into World War II, protected by oceans on both sides and with its vast industrial resources, managed to take the theories of a handful of young physicists from the laboratory to the battlefield in what became known as the Manhattan Project – and, as a result, change the nature of warfare and the world forever.

Chapter Two
Splitting the Atom

At the beginning of the 20th century, New Zealander Ernest Rutherford became interested in the radiation given off by radioactive materials. It came in three types: alpha, beta and gamma. It was alpha radiation that particularly interested him because it comprised particles of the tangible mass. These had a positive charge and, in 1907, he proved they were helium ions – that is, atoms of helium stripped of their electrons. At the time, atoms were thought to be solid objects with light-weight electrons embedded in a mass of positively charged material, like raisins in a pudding. This was known as the 'plum pudding' model.

At Manchester University, Rutherford – a chemist, although he became the father of nuclear physics – began firing alpha particles at a thin sheet of gold. These energetic particles should have passed straight through. However, some bounced back.

'It was almost as incredible as if you fired a fifteen-inch shell at a piece of tissue paper and it came back and hit you,' he said.

This meant that the atom could not be a uniform solid. Rather, it must be largely empty space with most of its mass concentrated in a tiny central nucleus, Rutherford realized in 1911. It was a mini-solar system. Two years later, Danish physicist Niels Bohr explained that while the chemical properties of the atom are due to the orbiting electrons, radioactivity lies in the nucleus.

In 1919, Rutherford discovered that by bombarding nitrogen with alpha particles you could change it into oxygen. This was the first artificial transmutation of an element, a process not thought possible outside alchemy. The process gave off positively charged particles, which he identified as the nuclei of hydrogen atoms, later called protons.

Returning to Cambridge as head of the Cavendish Laboratory, Rutherford continued to bombard various elements with alpha particles. With light elements he could produce similar transmutations, but with heavier elements the alpha particles were repelled by the higher positive charge on the nucleus. To investigate the nuclei of heavier elements, more energy was needed and particle accelerators were developed.

In 1932, James Chadwick, who Rutherford had brought to the Cavendish from Manchester, identified a third particle, the neutron, so named because it had no charge. This had been predicted by Rutherford and completed the picture of the atomic structure as we now know it.

The number of protons in the nucleus determined the element's atomic number. Hydrogen, with one proton, came first on the periodic table of elements and uranium, with 92 protons, came last. This simple scheme had become more complicated when chemists discovered that many elements existed at different atomic weights even while displaying identical chemical properties. Chadwick's discovery of the neutron explained this mystery. Atoms of the same element had different weights because they contained different numbers of neutrons. These differing atoms of the same element were called isotopes.

The three isotopes of uranium, for example, all have 92 protons in their nuclei and 92 electrons in orbit around them. But uranium-238, which comprises over 99 per cent of natural uranium, has 146 neutrons in its nucleus, compared with 143 neutrons in the rare uranium-235 (comprising 0.7 per cent of natural uranium) and 142 neutrons in uranium-234 (0.006 per cent). The slight difference in atomic weight between the uranium-235 and uranium-238 isotopes was an important factor in the making of the atomic bomb.

The year 1932 produced other notable events in atomic physics. Two of Rutherford's students, the Englishman John D. Cockcroft and the Irishman Ernest T. S. Walton, were the first to split the atom when they bombarded lithium with protons generated by a particle accelerator, causing the nucleus to split into two helium nuclei. That year, Ernest O. Lawrence and his colleagues M. Stanley Livingston and Milton White, on the Berkeley campus of the University of California, successfully operated the first cyclotron. This produced the high-energy particle beams needed for further nuclear research.

Moonshine

Lawrence's cyclotron, the Cockcroft-Walton machine and the Van de Graaff electrostatic generator, developed by Robert J. Van de Graaff at Princeton University, were types of particle accelerators designed to bombard the nuclei of various elements to disintegrate atoms. These early accelerators produced beams of either alpha particles or protons. Since alpha particles and protons are positively charged, they met substantial resistance from the positively charged target nucleus. Even high-speed protons and alpha particles scored a direct hit on a nucleus in only about one in a million times. Most simply passed by the target nucleus or were deflected.

The New Zealand-born chemist Ernest Rutherford (1871–1937).

Bombarding atoms this way was a useful method of furthering knowledge of nuclear physics. During such collisions, a small amount of matter would be lost, resulting in the release of huge amounts of energy given by Einstein's famous formula E= mc2. This showed the equivalence of mass and energy, where E is the energy, m is the mass and c is the speed of light, around 300,000 kilometres a second, or some 670 million an hour. So c2 is a very large number indeed.

But to Rutherford, Einstein and Bohr it was unlikely to harness the power of the atom for practical purposes any time in the near future. In a speech in 1933 – the year Hitler came to power in Germany – Rutherford called such expectations 'moonshine'. Einstein compared particle bombardment with shooting in the dark at scarce birds, while Bohr agreed that the chances of taming atomic energy were remote. The following year, the three Noble laureates were proved wrong.

Enrico Fermi

In 1934, working at Fascist dictator Benito Mussolini's Accademia d'Italia in Rome, Italian physicist Enrico Fermi began bombarding elements with neutrons instead of protons, figuring that Chadwick's uncharged particles could pass into the nucleus without resistance. Like other scientists at the time, Fermi paid little attention to the possibility that if he was successful, the experiment might result in a large amount of energy being given off – that is, an explosion.

Fermi and his colleagues bombarded 63 stable elements and produced 37 new radioactive isotopes. They also found that carbon and hydrogen proved useful as moderators in slowing the bombarding neutrons. While alpha particles and protons needed to be accelerated to high speeds to overcome the electrostatic repulsion from the nucleus, slow neutrons produced the best results as they remained in the vicinity of the nucleus longer and were consequently more likely to be captured.

One element Fermi bombarded with slow neutrons was uranium, the heaviest of the then known elements. Some scientists thought that the resulting transmutations produced new transuranic elements, while others noted that the chemical properties of the substances produced resembled those of lighter elements. Fermi himself was unsure. For the next few years, attempts to identify these substances dominated the research agenda of the international scientific community.

The answer came out of Nazi Germany just before Christmas 1938. By then, Fermi had fled Italy, which had introduced

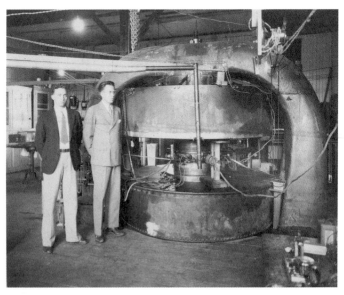

M. Stanley Livingston (L) and Ernest O. Lawrence in front of the 27-inch cyclotron at the old Radiation Laboratory at the University of California, Berkeley.

anti-Semitic race laws. He had been awarded the Nobel Prize for physics that year, and this gave him the excuse to take his Jewish wife and children to Sweden for the presentation. They travelled on to New York and used the prize money to establish themselves in the United States.

The discovery of fission

At the Kaiser Wilhelm Institute in Berlin, radio-chemists Otto Hahn and Fritz Strassmann were bombarding elements with neutrons when they made an unexpected discovery. They found that while the nuclei of most elements changed some-what during neutron bombardment, producing new isotopes, uranium nuclei changed greatly. But they did not produce the new transuranic elements that some thought Fermi had discovered. Instead they split, breaking into two roughly equal pieces. The products were a radioactive isotope of barium, atomic number 56, lanthanum, atomic number 57, and other elements from the middle of the periodic table.

What's more, the products of the Hahn-Strassmann experiment weighed less than the original uranium nuclei. It followed from Einstein's equation that the loss of mass resulting from the splitting process must have been converted into kinetic energy, which could in turn be converted into heat. Calculations made by Lise Meitner, a Jewish colleague who had fled to Sweden that summer, and her nephew, Otto Frisch, led to the conclusion that so much energy had been released that a previously undiscovered kind of process was at work. Borrowing the term for cell division in biology (binary fission), Frisch named the process fission. It seems that Fermi had produced fission in 1934 but had not realized it.

Chain reaction

The process of fission discovered by Hahn and Strassmann had another important characteristic besides the immediate release of enormous amounts of energy. This was the emission of neutrons. The energy released when fission occurred in uranium caused several neutrons to 'boil off' the two main fragments as they flew apart. Given the right set of circumstances, these secondary neutrons could collide with other nuclei, causing them to split and release more neutrons. These in turn might smash into other nuclei, with each interaction emitting energy.

Beginning with a single uranium nucleus, fission could not only produce substantial amounts of energy but could also lead to a chain reaction creating ever-increasing amounts of energy. This possibility completely altered the prospects for releasing the energy stored in the nucleus. A controlled self-sustaining reaction could make it possible to generate a large amount of energy for heat and power, while an unchecked reaction could create an explosion of tremendous force.

The idea that it would be possible to make an atomic bomb had already occurred to Leo Szilard. He had worked alongside Einstein at the Institute of Technology in Berlin, where they had patented an electromagnet refrigeration pump that had no moving parts. The design was sold to AEG, who made one, but it was too noisy to use and never got beyond the prototype.

Szilard was a fan of H. G. Wells and travelled to London in 1929 to meet him and buy the Central European rights for his book *The Open Conspiracy*. In 1932, Szilard read *The World Set Free*. Though written nearly 20 years earlier, it described an atomic bomb of immense power that would destroy the major cities of the world.

In 1933, Szilard was again in London, this time a Jewish

refugee from Nazi Germany. He was staying at the Imperial Hotel in Russell Square. On 12 September 1933, after reading Rutherford's 'moonshine' speech in *The Times*, he was crossing Southampton Row at the south side of Russell Square when suddenly the idea of the chain reaction came to him and, with it, the possibility of making a bomb.

He patented the idea. Then in 1936, fearing that concept would fall into Nazi hands, he assigned the patent to the British Admiralty to ensure its secrecy. Two years later, he moved to New York to join Fermi.

Fission comes to America

Lise Meitner and Otto Frisch communicated their results to Niels Bohr in Copenhagen just as he was preparing to leave for the US, where he and Fermi were to open the Fifth Washington Conference on Theoretical Physics. Bohr confirmed the validity of the findings while sailing to New York, arriving on 16 January 1939. Ten days later Bohr, accompanied by Fermi, informed a number of European émigré scientists who had sought refuge in America. The American scientific community was let in on the secret at the opening session of the conference.

American physicists quickly grasped the importance of Bohr's news. Lawrence's cyclotron had made Berkeley Radiation Laboratory the unofficial capital of nuclear physics in the US. Lawrence, Van de Graaff and other Americans now led the way in producing equipment for nuclear physics and high-energy physics research. They quickly set about confirming and developing Hahn and Strassmann's results. Meanwhile, Bohr and John A. Wheeler advanced the theory of fission at Princeton, while Fermi and Szilard collaborated with Walter H. Zinn and Herbert L. Anderson at Columbia

University, where they investigated the possibility of producing a nuclear chain reaction.

It was already known that when uranium fissioned it emitted neutrons – usually two. So the question was, under what conditions was a chain reaction in uranium possible? And in which of the three isotopes of the heavy metal was it most likely to occur?

Otto Hahn and Lise Meitner in the laboratory, 1913.

Uranium-235

By March 1940, John R. Dunning and his colleagues at Columbia, in collaboration with Alfred O. Nier of the University of Minnesota, had demonstrated conclusively that uranium-235 was the isotope that fissioned with slow neutrons, rather than more abundant uranium-238 as Fermi had thought. This meant that a chain reaction using the slightly lighter uranium-235 was possible, but only if the isotope could be separated from the uranium-238 and concentrated into a critical mass – that is, a mass big enough for neutrons to stand a good chance of striking another nucleus, causing the release of more neutrons and a self-sustaining, chain reaction before they left the material.

However, as U-235 was present in only 1 in 140 parts in natural uranium, the process of separating enough of it posed serious problems. So Fermi continued to try to make a chain reaction using large amounts of natural uranium that he called a 'pile'. This was thought to have come from the Italian word *pila*, the name the Italian scientist Conte Alessandro Volta had given the first electric battery. However, Fermi maintained that he had simply used the English word 'pile', meaning a heap.

Dunning's and Nier's work with U-235 showed that it was possible to generate nuclear power, but not necessarily that it was possible to make a bomb. It was already known that a bomb would require fission by the fast neutrons produced by fission itself. To produce slow neutrons, fast neutrons had to undergo a number of collisions, so a chain reaction produced by slow neutrons might not proceed very far before the metal would blow itself apart, causing little, if any, damage.

U-238 fissioned with fast neutrons, but could not sustain a chain reaction because it required neutrons with higher energy than those produced naturally. The crucial question was whether U-235 could fission with fast neutrons to produce a chain reaction. However, at that point, scientists had not isolated enough U-235 to perform the experiments necessary to find out.

The Uranium Committee

President Roosevelt responded to Einstein's letter by setting up the Advisory Committee on Uranium under Lyman J. Briggs, director of the National Bureau of Standards. It met for the first time on 21 October 1939. The committee was to look into the current state of research on uranium to recommend an appropriate role for the federal government. In early 1940, the Uranium Committee recommended that the government fund Fermi's and Szilard's work on chain reactions at Columbia, as well as limited research on isotope separation.

To test whether U-235 would fission with fast neutrons it was necessary to separate it from naturally occurring uranium. But as U-235 and U-238 were chemically identical – differing only in the number of neutrons they had in the nucleus – they could not be separated by chemical means. And as their masses differed by less than 1 per cent, separation by physical means would be extremely difficult and expensive. Nevertheless, several methods were tried.

Nier at the University of Minnesota pioneered an electromagnetic method. This used a mass spectrometer, or spectrograph, which sent a stream of ionized uranium atoms through a magnetic field. Atoms of the lighter isotope would be deflected more by the magnetic field than those of the heavier isotope, so the stream would split in two. The two resulting branches could then be collected at two separate points. However, the electromagnetic method, as it existed in 1940,

Creator of the first nuclear reactor Enrico Fermi (1901–54).

would have taken far too long to have been any use in the war. To separate 1 gram of U-235, using a single mass spectrometer, would have taken 27,000 years.

Gaseous diffusion seemed more promising. It was based on the well-known principle that molecules of a lighter isotope would pass through a porous barrier more easily than molecules of a heavier one. The approach proposed would call for the process to be repeated many times, each enriching the proportion of U-235 in the sample slightly as it travelled through a series of cascades. Theoretically, this process could achieve high concentrations of U-235 but, like the electromagnetic method, would be extremely costly. British researchers had already been at work on gaseous diffusion, John R. Dunning and his colleagues at Columbia joining them in late 1940.

Many scientists thought the best hope for isotope separation was the high-speed centrifuge, a device based on the same principle as the cream separator. A gaseous mixture of natural uranium would be spun at high speed. Centrifugal force would throw the heavier U-238 to the outside, leaving the lighter U-235 to be drawn off at the centre. Again, the process would have to be repeated many times, enriching the sample a little each time. But a cascade system of hundreds, if not thousands, of centrifuges could produce a sufficiently rich mixture. This method, which was pursued primarily by Jesse W. Beams at the University of Virginia, received much of the early isotope separation funding.

The Uranium Committee briefly showed an interest in a fourth enrichment process called liquid thermal diffusion. This was being investigated by Philip H. Abelson at the Carnegie Institution in Washington, DC. Abelson placed pressurized liquid uranium hexafluoride in the space between two concentric vertical pipes. The inner wall was heated by with high-pressure steam, while the outer wall was cooled by water

circulating through a water jacket. It was found that the lighter
isotope tended to concentrate near the hot wall and the
heavier near the cold. Convection would in time carry the
lighter isotope to the top of the column and taller columns
would produce more separation. Like other enrichment
methods, liquid thermal diffusion was at an early stage of
development, but the Uranium Committee soon decided that
it was not worth pursuing.

The pile

In 1934, Fermi had demonstrated the value of moderators in
producing slow neutrons. He thought that a mixture of natural
uranium and the right moderator could produce a self-
sustaining chain reaction. Both Fermi and Szilard favoured
carbon in the form of graphite as a moderator. The graphite
could moderate, or slow down, the neutrons coming from the
fission reaction, increasing the probability of their causing
additional fissions and, perhaps, initiating the chain reaction.
A pile containing a large amount of natural uranium could then
produce enough secondary neutrons to keep a reaction going,
they thought.

Though it was far from certain that this would work, in
their first report, issued on 1 November 1939, the Uranium
Committee recommended that the government should immediately obtain 4 tons of graphite and 50 tons of uranium oxide.
This would cost and, in February 1940, would be the first
outlay of government funds. It reflected the importance
attached to the Fermi-Szilard pile experiments already
underway at Columbia University.

Again, there was a huge theoretical difference between
building a self-generating pile and making a bomb. However,
the pile envisioned by Fermi and Szilard could produce large

President Roosevelt's response to Albert Einstein after he eventually received Einstein's letter of 2 August.

My dear Professor:

I want to thank you for your recent letter and the most interesting and important enclosure.

I found this data of such import that I have convened a Board consisting of the head of the Bureau of Standards and a chosen representative of the Army and Navy to thoroughly investigate the possibilities of your suggestion regarding the element of uranium.

I am glad to say that Dr. Sachs will cooperate and work with this Committee and I feel this is the most practical and effective method of dealing with the subject.

Please accept my sincere thanks.

Very sincerely yours,

[Franklin D Roosevelt]

amounts of power and might have military applications, such as powering naval vessels. Even if such a pile could be triggered to explode, it was much too big to make a practical bomb. The separation of U-235 or substantial enrichment of natural uranium with U-235 was what was needed to create the fast-neutron reaction on a small enough scale to make a usable bomb. While Fermi was confident of success in generating energy with his graphite power pile, he thought that there was 'little likelihood of an atomic bomb, little proof that we were not pursuing a chimera'.

Chapter Three
Science Goes to War

As war engulfed Europe, Vannevar Bush, president of the
Carnegie Foundation, was one of the many people in the
United States who became convinced that their country would
inevitably become involved. Science must be mobilized and, in
June 1940, Roosevelt established the National Defense
Research Committee with Bush at its head. Its priorities were
the development of radar, proximity fuses and anti-submarine
devices. The Uranium Committee fell under its remit. It was
reconstituted as a scientific body and purged of its military
membership. In the interest of security, foreign-born scientists
were barred from the committee and further publication of
articles on uranium research was banned.

Ernest Lawrence was another of those convinced that it was
merely a matter of time before the US was drawn into World
War II, and he wanted the government to mobilize its scientific
forces as rapidly as possible. Specifically, what Lawrence had
on his mind in early 1941 were experiments taking place in his
own laboratory, using samples produced by bombarding
uranium with the cyclotron. Studying uranium fission fragments, Edwin M. McMillan and Philip H. Abelson identified
element 93, neptunium. This was the first transuranic – that is,

man-made – element. Then Glenn T. Seaborg discovered that
an isotope of neptunium decayed to yet another transuranic
element – element 94, which he later named plutonium. He
found that plutonium-239 was 1.7 times as likely as U-235 to
fission. This was an important development as the Fermi-
Szilard pile could produce large amounts of fissionable plutonium from the plentiful U-238, which could then be separated
chemically. It promised to be a less expensive and simpler
process than building isotope-separation plants.

Lawrence then had to convert his smaller cyclotron into a
spectrograph to separate U-235. He contacted Karl T. Compton
and Alfred L. Loomis at Harvard University, who were both
doing radar work for the National Defense Research
Committee. Compton forwarded Lawrence's optimistic assessment of uranium research to Bush, warning that Germany was
undoubtedly making progress. The Uranium Committee were
dragging their feet and Compton noted that the British
researchers were ahead of their US colleagues, though they
lacked America's resources.

Funding

After a meeting in New York, Bush decided to appoint
Lawrence as an advisor to Briggs. As a result, funding was
provided for plutonium work at Berkeley and for Nier's mass
spectrograph at Minnesota. The National Academy of Sciences
was then to review the uranium research programme. A
committee headed by Arthur Compton of the University of
Chicago and also including Lawrence submitted a report on
17 May 1941. It concluded that increased uranium funding
could produce radioactive material that could be dropped on
an enemy by 1943, a pile that could power naval vessels could
be developed in three or four years and a bomb of enormous

power could be built at some point in the future, but certainly not before 1945.

Even practical-minded Bush was not impressed. He asked the National Academy of Sciences to reassess its findings from an engineering standpoint. In a second report on 11 July, it admitted that it could promise no immediate applications. Once again Bush was disappointed.

By the time Bush received the National Academy of Sciences' second report, he had been appointed director of the Office of Scientific Research and Development. This had been established by an executive order on 28 June 1941 – six days after German troops invaded the Soviet Union – giving Bush direct access to the White House. The National Defense Research Committee, now headed by James B. Conant, president of Harvard University, was downgraded to an advisory body while the Uranium Committee became a section of the OSRD, codenamed S-1 – Section One of the Office of Scientific Research and Development.

The MAUD Report

Bush's disappointment with the 11 July National Academy of Sciences report did not last long. Several days later he and Conant received a copy of a draft report forwarded from the National Defense Research Committee liaison office in London. The MAUD report came from the Military Application of Uranium Detonation Committee set up by the British in the spring of 1940 to study the possibility of developing a nuclear weapon. Refugee physicists Rudolf Peierls and Otto Frisch, working at Birmingham University, maintained that a sufficiently purified critical mass of U-235 could fission even with fast neutrons. They estimated that a critical mass of 22 pounds would be large enough to produce an enormous explosion.

The electrical engineer Vannevar Bush (1890-1974) who became Director of the US Office of Scientific Research & Development.

A bomb that size could be loaded on existing aircraft and be ready in around two years.

The Americans had been following the workings of the MAUD Committee since the autumn of 1940. Its distinguished scientists had high credibility with not just Bush and Conant, but with Roosevelt himself. Here at last were specific plans for producing an atomic bomb.

While the British believed that uranium research could lead to the production of a bomb in time to affect the outcome of the war, the MAUD report dismissed plutonium production, thermal diffusion, the electromagnetic method and centrifuges. It called for the use of gaseous diffusion of U-235 on a massive scale. It also reminded the Americans that fission had been discovered in Nazi Germany nearly three years earlier, and since spring 1940, a large part of the Kaiser Wilhelm Institute in Berlin had been set aside for uranium research.

Encouraged, Bush and Conant strengthened the Uranium Committee, adding Fermi as head of theoretical studies and Harold C. Urey, another Nobel laureate, as head of isotope separation and heavy water research. Heavy water – that is, water containing the hydrogen isotope deuterium – had been discovered by Urey in 1931. It was considered a useful moderator and the Germans were getting their supply from the Norsk-Hydro plant in Norway, later sabotaged by the British Special Operations Executive.

Bush asked yet another National Academy of Sciences committee to re-evaluate the uranium programme. This time he gave Compton specific instructions to address technical questions of critical mass and destructive capability, and to verify the MAUD results.

Without waiting for Compton's committee to finish its work, Bush went to see Roosevelt on 9 October. He summarized the British findings and discussed the cost of building a bomb and how long it might take, though he was still by no means convinced it could be done.

Roosevelt gave his permission for Bush to discuss the construction of a bomb with the Army. He was to move ahead as quickly as possible, but not to go beyond research and development without presidential authorization. Roosevelt indicated that he would find a way to finance the project if it proved feasible, and he asked Bush to draft a letter to the British government, enlisting their co-operation.

Pearl Harbor

Compton reported back on 6 November, just one month and a day before the Japanese attack on Pearl Harbor on 7 December

1941 brought the United States into World War II, with Germany and Italy declaring war on the US on 10 December. Compton's committee concluded that a critical mass of between 4½ and 220 pounds of U-235 would produce a powerful fission bomb. The cost of isotope separation alone would be $50–100 million.

While the National Academy of Sciences committee was less optimistic than the British, it confirmed the basic conclusions of the MAUD committee. Bush forwarded their findings to Roosevelt under a cover letter on 27 November. Roosevelt did not reply until 19 January 1942. When he did, it was as commander in chief of a nation at war. The president's hand-written note read simply: 'V. B. OK – returned – I think you had best keep this in your own safe. FDR.'

Ever eager, Bush had not waited for Roosevelt's response. He had already put Eger V. Murphree, a chemical engineer with the Standard Oil Company, in charge of a group responsible for overseeing engineering studies and supervising pilot plant construction and any laboratory-scale investigations. He appointed Urey, Lawrence and Compton as programme chiefs.

Urey was to head up work on diffusion and centrifuge methods and heavy-water studies. Lawrence took the studies of electromagnetic methods and plutonium, while Compton ran chain-reaction and weapon-theory programmes. Bush's own responsibility was to co-ordinate scientific and engineering efforts and make final decisions when it came to awarding construction contracts.

Under instructions from Roosevelt, the responsibility for all work concerning uranium was taken from the National Defense Research Committee and given to the newly constituted Top Policy Group, which comprised Bush, Conant, Vice President Henry A. Wallace, Secretary of War Henry L. Stimson and Army Chief of Staff George C. Marshall. A high-level conference convened by Wallace on 16 December put the seal of approval on these arrangements. Two days later, the S-1 Committee gave Lawrence $400,000 to continue his electromagnetic work.

With the US now at war and fearing that the American effort to build a bomb lagged behind Nazi Germany's, American scientists were gripped with a renewed sense of urgency. While Bush fine-tuned the organizational apparatus, new scientific information poured in from laboratories. This had to be analysed ready to be incorporated into the planning for the upcoming design and construction stage.

In May 1942, American naval forces won their first important victory in the Battle of the Coral Sea, checking the Japanese advance in the Pacific. The US was now on a full war footing. Money was no object and the race for the bomb was on.

Isotope separation

During the first half of 1942, several routes to a bomb were explored. At Columbia, Urey worked on the gaseous diffusion and centrifuge systems for isotope separation in the code-named SAM – Substitute or Special Alloy Metals – Laboratory. At Berkeley, Lawrence continued his investigations into electromagnetic separation using the mass spectrometer he had converted from his 37-inch cyclotron. Compton marshalled facilities at the University of Chicago's Metallurgical Laboratory for pile experiments aimed at producing plutonium. Meanwhile, Murphree began work on production facilities.

His group was also in charge of sourcing uranium ore. It was estimated that some 150 tons would be needed through mid-1944. Then it was discovered that some 1,250 tons of pitchblende high-grade, 65 per cent uranium oxide mined by the Belgians in the Congo, were stored on Staten Island, and Murphree made arrangements to get additional supplies from

The U.S. Navy battleships USS West Virginia (BB-48) (sunken, left) and USS Tennessee (BB-43) shrouded in smoke following the Japanese air raid on Pearl Harbor on 7 December 1941.

the Colorado Plateau, America's only source, and Canada.

Uranium hexafluoride was also needed for the centrifuge and the gaseous and thermal diffusion processes. Abelson, now with the Naval Research Laboratory, was producing small quantities, and Murphree made arrangements with DuPont and the Harshaw Chemical Company of Cleveland to produce hexafluoride on a scale sufficient to keep the vital isotope separation research going.

Lawrence was so successful in producing enriched samples of U-235 electromagnetically with his converted cyclotron that Bush sent a special progress report to Roosevelt on 9 March 1942. He told the president that Lawrence's work might lead to a short cut to the bomb, especially in light of new calculations indicating that the critical mass required might well be smaller than previously thought. The weapon would probably be more powerful and Bush believed that if matters were expedited, it would be possible to build a bomb by 1944. Two days later the president responded: 'I think the whole thing should be pushed not only in regard to development, but also with due regard to time. This is very much of the essence.'

However, isotope separation studies using centrifuges at Columbia hit serious engineering difficulties. Not only were the specifications for the centrifuge demanding, but, depending upon rotor size, it was estimated that tens of thousands of centrifuges would be needed to produce enough U-235. Gaseous diffusion also ran into trouble. The barrier had to be a corrosion-resistant membrane with millions of sub-microscopic holes per square inch. Both separation methods demanded the design and construction of parts never before produced, finished to tolerances never previously achieved by American industry. Seemingly, new technologies would have to be created overnight.

Stagg Field

Initially, Compton had funded Fermi's pile at Columbia, along with Seaborg's plutonium studies in Berkeley and the theoretical work of Eugene Wigner at Princeton and J. Robert Oppenheimer at Berkeley, while Szilard was head of materials acquisition. Then in April 1942, Compton began to centralize everything in Chicago.

He took space wherever he could find it. In a racket court under the west grandstand at Stagg Field, Samuel K. Allison began work building a graphite and uranium pile. While it was recognized that heavy water was a better moderator than graphite, the only available supply was a small amount that the British had smuggled out of France before the Germans invaded in 1940. So, in the new climate of urgency, Compton decided to go ahead with graphite, as both Allison and Fermi, still at Columbia, were getting good results. Meanwhile, fresh theoretical work cast doubt on the MAUD report's negative assessment of plutonium and Compton hoped that Allison's pile would provide enough plutonium to make a weapon.

By May 1942, with scientific work forging ahead, Bush turned his mind to production. He instructed Conant and the leaders of S-1 to make recommendations on all ways to make a bomb, regardless of cost. Assessing the progress of the four methods of isotope separation then under consideration – gaseous diffusion, centrifuge, electromagnetic and the pile – the committee could not pick a front-runner and recommended that all be pushed forwards as fast as possible. With funds readily available and the outcome of the war far from decided, the S-1 leadership recommended that all four methods proceed to the pilot-plant stage and full production planning.

The Corps of Engineers

Clearly the question of security was a high priority, so it was suggested that the S-1 project should be put under the control of one of the armed forces. Clearly, the army, with its Corps of Engineers, was most suitable. Roosevelt had approved army involvement on 9 October 1941, and army officers joined S-1 meetings in March 1942. On 23 May, the Corps of Engineers was called in to build the necessary production facilities.

The responsibility for process development, materials procurement, engineering design and site selection would now fall to the Corps of Engineers. As a result, the Corps would get around 60 per cent of the proposed budget, or $54 million, earmarked for 1943. An army officer would be put in overall command of the entire project.

The remaining $30 million would be left with S-1 for university research and pilot plant studies. An S-1 Executive Committee, comprising Conant, Briggs, Compton, Lawrence, Murphree and Urey, would oversee all Office of Scientific Research and Development work and keep abreast of technical developments that might influence engineering considerations or plant design. However, the nature of the American atomic bomb effort changed from one dominated by research scientists to an enterprise run by the military.

Chapter Four
The Military Move In

In the summer of 1942, US forces began their island-hopping campaign across the Pacific at Guadalcanal in the Solomon Islands. Meanwhile, under the army take-over of the atomic bomb programme, Colonel James C. Marshall, a West Point graduate with experience of building air bases, was put in charge of the new Laboratory for the Development of Substitute Metals, or DSM. In New York City, Marshall set up the Manhattan Engineer District, or MED. This was established by general order on 13 August. Marshall, like the majority of army officers, knew nothing of nuclear physics. He moved cautiously, delaying the purchase of a production site in Tennessee pending further study, though the scientists who had been involved in the project from the start were pressing for immediate purchase.

While Bush had carefully managed the transition to army control, there was not yet a mechanism to arbitrate disagreements between S-1 and the military. There was bound to be a falling out. In June 1942, Marshall had a conversation with Norman Hilberry, Compton's top assistant and an expert in cosmic rays.

'Now look, Hilberry,' said Marshall. 'There is clearly a major misunderstanding here that has got to be straightened out. It seems to us that all you folk are thinking in terms of making one or two bombs. Isn't that true?'

Hilberry confirmed this, explaining that the scientists believed that if the atomic bomb worked at all, it would be so incredibly destructive that just one or two would be enough to win the war. The psychological impact on the enemy of such wholesale destruction would make them surrender immediately.

'That's all wrong,' said Marshall. 'There is a fundamental principle in military matters which – and I don't care how fantastic this atomic device may prove to be – is not going to be violated. This is one's ability to continue delivering the weapon, and it's this that determines whether the weapon is useful. If you folks succeeded in making only one bomb, I can assure you it would never be used. The only basic principle on which the military can operate is the ability to continue to deliver. You've got to sit down and get re-orientated. The thing we're talking about is not a number of bombs; what we are talking about is production capacity to continue delivering bombs at given rate. That, you will discover, is a very different problem.'

Hilberry reported this to the scientists in Chicago. They still refused to believe that more than a couple of bombs would be necessary. The materials needed to make a bomb were scarce. Setting up a production line to mass-produce them was out of the question and the resulting lack of co-ordination put the future of the entire bomb project in question.

Szilard was beside himself.

'In 1939,' he wrote in a memo to Bush, 'the government of the United States was give a unique opportunity by providence; this opportunity was lost. Nobody can tell now whether we shall be ready before German bombs wipe out American cities. Such scanty information as we have about work in Germany is not reassuring and all one can say with certainty is that we could move at least twice as fast if our difficulties were eliminated.'

The difficulties he identified were that the programme was organized along authoritarian rather than democratic lines.

General Groves

Clearly, someone other than Marshall needed to be put in charge of the Manhattan Engineer District, which became commonly known at the Manhattan Project. On 17 September 1942, the army appointed Colonel Leslie R. Groves. He was promoted to brigadier general six days later. Groves was an engineer with impressive credentials, including the building of the Pentagon, and, most importantly, had strong administrative abilities. Within two days of his appointment Groves acted to obtain the Tennessee site and secured a higher priority rating for project materials. In addition, he moved the Manhattan Engineer District headquarters from New York to Washington to gain better access to other federal agencies. He quickly recognized the talents of Marshall's deputy, Colonel Kenneth D. Nichols, and arranged for Nichols to work as his chief aide and trouble-shooter throughout the war.

Nichols said that Groves was 'the biggest S.O.B. I have ever worked for. He is most demanding. He is most critical. He is always a driver, never a praiser. He is abrasive and sarcastic. He disregards all normal organizational channels. He is extremely intelligent. He has the guts to make timely, difficult decisions. He is the most egotistical man I know. He knows he is right and so sticks by his decision. He abounds with energy and expects everyone to work as hard, or even harder, than he does . . . if I had to do my part of the atomic bomb project over again and had the privilege of picking my boss, I would pick General Groves.'

On 5 October 1942, Groves paid his first visit to the Metallurgical Laboratory in Chicago to meet Compton, Fermi,

British physicist Sir James Chadwick (left), working with American scientists.

Wigner, Szilard, Hilberry and ten other top scientists who were working there.

'As the meeting was drawing to a close, I asked the question that is always uppermost in the mind of an engineer,' Groves said. 'With respect to the amount of fissionable material needed for each bomb, how accurate did they think their estimate was? I expected a reply of 'within 25 or 50 per cent', and would not have been greatly surprised at an even greater percentage, but I was horrified when they quite blandly replied that they thought it was correct within a factor of ten.'

This meant that if they thought they needed 100 pounds of plutonium to make one bomb, the real amount could be anywhere from 10 pounds to 1000.

'My position could be compared to that of a caterer who is told he must be prepared to serve anywhere between 10 and 1000 guests,' Groves said. 'It completely destroyed any thought of reasonable planning for the production plants for fissionable material.'

But good news was just around the corner. While it had been theoretically possible to transmute U-238 into plutonium, experimental proof was obtained on 2 December 1942.

'This was weeks after we had decided to go ahead at full speed with the plutonium process, and many days after we had started to prepare the plans for a major plant,' said Groves.

The Military Policy Committee

With the help and authority of Secretary of War Henry L. Stimson, Bush set up the Military Policy Committee, which included a representative each from the army, the navy and the Office of Scientific Research and Development. Bush hoped that scientists would have better access to decision-making in the new structure than they had when DSM and S-1 operated as parallel but separate units. With Groves in overall command and the Military Policy Committee in place, Bush felt that early organizational deficiencies had been remedied. The Top Policy Group retained broad policy authority, while Marshall remained as District Engineer, a role where his cautious nature would prove useful later.

During the summer and autumn of 1942, administrative and technical difficulties remained formidable. Each of the four isotope separation processes were still under consideration, but a full-scale commitment to all four posed serious problems, even with the project's high priority.

When Groves took command in mid-September, he made it clear that by late 1942 decisions would be made about which path promised to produce a bomb in the shortest time. The demands of war meant scientists had to move from laboratory research to development and production in record time.

Although traditional scientific caution might be bypassed in the process, there was no alternative if a bomb was to be built in time to be used in the current conflict. Everyone involved in the Manhattan Project soon learned that Groves never lost sight of this goal and all his decisions were made accordingly.

Decision time

Groves was determined to make good on his timetable when he scheduled a meeting of the Military Policy Committee on 12 November and a meeting of the S-1 Executive Committee two days later. The scientists doing isotope separation research knew these meetings would determine which separation method would be used. There was keen competition. Lawrence and his staff at Berkeley had edged the electromagnetic method into the lead. The S-1 Executive Committee even toyed with the idea of using all its money to bank Lawrence, but was persuaded not to by Conant.

Throughout the summer and autumn, Lawrence refined his new 184-inch magnet and huge cyclotron to make the first calutron. Named for the University of California – Cal. U. – this was a mass spectrometer designed specifically for the separation of U-235. The S-1 Executive Committee visited Berkeley on 13 September and subsequently recommended building both a pilot plant and a large section of a full-scale plant in Tennessee.

The centrifuge being developed by Jesse Beams at the University of Virginia was the big loser in the November meetings. Westinghouse had been unable to overcome problems with its model centrifuge. Parts failed due to severe vibrations during trial runs, so a pilot plant and the possibility of going into production appeared impractical in the near future. Conant had already concluded that the centrifuge was likely to be dropped when he reported to Bush on 26 October.

Gaseous diffusion held some promise and remained a live option, although the Dunning group at Columbia had yet to produce any U-235 by the November meetings. The major problem was still the barrier. Nickel was considered the best barrier material, but there was serious doubt whether enough reliable nickel barriers could be produced by the end of the war.

While gaseous diffusion received mixed reviews, proponents of the pile in Chicago remained optimistic. However, shortages of both uranium and graphite delayed construction of the Stagg Field pile – Chicago Pile Number One of CP-1, as it was known. But now Fermi had moved to Chicago and all pile research was being done there, it was thought that a successful experiment could be completed by the end of the year.

Further optimism stemmed from Seaborg's work with plutonium, particularly when he found that, by oxidizing the metal, it could separate plutonium from the uranium remaining in the pile. In August 1942, Seaborg's team produced a micro-scopic sample of pure plutonium. This was a major chemical achievement, fully justifying further work on the pile.

However, the scientists were disappointed when they learned that construction and operation of the production facil-ities, now to be built near the Clinch River in Tennessee at Site X, would be turned over to a private firm. An experimental pile would be built also in the Argonne Forest Preserve just outside Chicago, but again the Metallurgical Laboratory scientists would have to cede their claim to pile technology to an organization experienced in construction to take the process into operation.

The luminaries

While the four isotope separation processes fought it out, theoretical studies were being undertaken that would also influence the decisions made in November. Robert Oppenheimer

Director of the Manhattan Project, Robert Oppenheimer (1904-67).

headed the work of a group of theoretical physicists he called 'the luminaries'. These included Felix Bloch, Hans Bethe, Edward Teller and Robert Serber, while John H. Manley assisted him by co-ordinating nationwide fission research and the instrument and measurement studies from the Metallurgical Laboratory in Chicago.

Despite inconsistent experimental results, the consensus emerging at Berkeley was that approximately twice as much fissionable material would be required for a bomb than had been thought six months earlier. This was disturbing, especially in light of the military's view that it would take more than one bomb to win the war. The goal of mass-producing fissionable material, which always seemed questionable, appeared even more unrealistic.

However, Oppenheimer did report, with some enthusiasm, that fusion explosions using deuterium – heavy hydrogen – might be possible. While the fission bomb depended on a heavy nucleus, such as that of uranium or plutonium breaking apart, a fusion bomb worked by fusing the nuclei of light atoms, such as hydrogen or deuterium, together. The possibility of making thermonuclear, or fusion, bombs was the immediate cause of optimism since deuterium supplies, while not abundant, were certainly larger and more easily replenished than were those of U-236 and plutonium. So S-1 authorized basic research on the use of light elements.

DuPont's doubts

The final input for the November meetings of the Military Policy Committee and the S-1 Executive Committee would come from DuPont. Groves had began courting the chemical giant when he took over the Manhattan Project in September, hoping that the company would undertake construction and operation of the plutonium separation plant in Tennessee. He appealed to the company's patriotism – the bomb project had high priority with the president and a successful effort could affect the outcome of the war.

DuPont managers showed little enthusiasm, but agreed to undertake an appraisal of the pile project. Noting that it was not even known if the chain reaction would work, DuPont said that, under the most favourable circumstances, plutonium could be mass-produced by 1945, though it emphasized that it thought the chances of this happening were low. This appraisal did not discourage Groves, who was confident that DuPont would take the assignment if it was offered.

Decision time

The Military Policy Committee met on 12 November 1942. Acting on Groves's and Conant's recommendations, it cancelled the centrifuge project. Gaseous diffusion, the electromagnetic method and the pile were to proceed directly to full-scale production, eliminating any pilot plant stage. The S-1 Executive Committee ratified these decisions two days later. It also agreed that the gaseous diffusion facility was of lower priority than either the pile or the electromagnetic plant, but it was ahead of the building of a second pile, which was already being discussed.

The scientific committee also asked DuPont to look into methods for increasing America's supplies of heavy water in case it was needed to serve as a moderator for one of the new piles.

Before anything went ahead, there was a brief scare. Neither Groves nor the S-1 Executive had been told that Compton was building the experimental pile at Stagg Field. They were faced with the vision of a chain reaction possibly running wild in heavily populated Chicago.

However, Fermi's calculations provided reasonable assurance that this was not going to happen. Information from British scientists then raised serious questions about the feasibility of deriving plutonium from the pile. It took several days for Groves and a committee of scientists, including Lawrence and Oppenheimer, to satisfy themselves completely that the pile experiment posed little danger and would in all probability produce plutonium as predicted.

Before finally going ahead, Groves appointed Warren K. Lewis of the Massachusetts Institute of Technology to head a final review committee on 18 November. It comprised himself and three representatives from DuPont. Over the next two weeks, the committee travelled from New York to Chicago to Berkeley and back again through Chicago. It endorsed the work on gaseous diffusion at Columbia, though it made some organizational recommendations. Indeed, the Lewis Committee recommended that gaseous diffusion should be elevated to first priority and expressed reservations about the electromagnetic programme, despite an impassioned presentation by Lawrence in Berkeley.

Building the pile

At Columbia, Fermi had already been working on the designs of possible reactors. To create a chain reaction, the neutrons given off by one fission must hit a second nucleus, causing it to fission and so on. But some of the neutrons would escape from the pile without hitting another uranium nucleus. Others would be captured by impurities in the uranium or by the moderator, so they would not be available to trigger another fission.

It was necessary to quantify this, so scientists came up with what they called the multiplication factor, k. This was the ratio of fissions in one step, or nuclear generation, in the chain to the number in the preceding generation. If k was less than one, any chain reaction would fizzle out. But if $k=1$, a chain reaction would be maintained and if k was greater than one, the reactor risked going supercritical with the chain reaction running out of control.

However, at that time it was not known whether a value for k greater than one could ever be obtained. If the Nazis had been able to determine this, they would have been well on the way towards producing an atomic bomb.

One of the first things that had to be determined was how best to place the uranium in the reactor to get k greater than one. Fermi and Szilard suggested placing the uranium in a cubic lattice of the moderating material, slowing the neutrons. This placement appeared to offer the best chance for a neutron to encounter a uranium atom. Graphite was picked as the moderator because it was the only one that could be obtained in sufficient quantity of the desired degree of purity.

The first pile

The first pile that Fermi built in Schermerhorn Hall on the campus at Columbia in September 1941 comprised cans of uranium oxide surrounded by graphite bricks. Its k was 0.87.

'That is by 0.13 less than one,' said Fermi – 13 per cent less than the minimum necessary to get the chain reaction going – 'and it was bad. However, at the moment we had a firm point to start from, and we had essentially to see whether we could squeeze the extra 0.13, or preferably a little bit more.'

Early in 1942 the Columbia and Princeton groups were transferred to Chicago where the Metallurgical Laboratory was established. There, work continued on some 13 subcritical-size piles – that is, ones that would not sustain a chain reaction.

By July 1942, they had edged k up to 0.918, then 0.94. Now they had measurements necessary to design a test pile of critical size.

However, in May 1942, one of the experimental piles reached a k of 0.995 and it was thought that it could be put above 1.0 if higher quality graphite could be obtained and uranium metal were used instead of uranium oxide as it was denser. Until then it was necessary to use uranium oxides because metallic uranium of the desired degree of purity did not exist.

Although several manufacturers were attempting to produce the uranium metal, it was not until November that any appreciable amount was available. By mid-November, several tons of the highly purified metal had been delivered. This was to be placed in the pile, as close to the centre as possible.

Constructing the main pile

Construction of the main pile in Chicago started in November. First the graphite blocks had to be machined and the uranium oxide pressed into pellets, while a separate team designed the instruments. Fermi's two construction crews, one under Zinn and the other under Anderson, toiled around the clock. Work on the instrumentation was headed by Volney 'Bill' Wilson, who had returned to Chicago from the secret radar project at MIT to work on the atomic bomb, despite his pacifism. Like many of the scientists working on the Manhattan project, he believed that the bomb would make future wars impossible.

As it was still not known whether the pile they had designed was big enough to go critical, it was decided to enclose it in a large cloth balloon, so that the air could be pumped out. The gases in air, like impurities in graphite and uranium, also capture neutrons. This balloon cloth bag was made by Goodyear Tire and Rubber Company. The company's engineers were specialists at making gasbags for lighter-than-air craft and were a little puzzled about the aerodynamics of a square balloon; however, because of security regulations, Goodyear could not be told the purpose of the Army's odd-shaped device.

The bag was hung up with one side left open, then a circular layer of graphite bricks was placed in the centre. This and each succeeding layer of the pile was braced by a wooden frame. Alternate layers contained the uranium. By this layer-on-layer method a roughly spherical pile of uranium and graphite would be constructed.

'We found out how coal miners feel,' said one of Zinn's group. 'After eight hours of machining graphite, we looked as if we were made up for a minstrel. One shower would remove only the surface graphite dust. About a half-hour after the first shower the dust in the pores of your skin would start oozing. Walking around the room where we cut the graphite was like walking on a dance floor. Graphite is a dry lubricant, you know, and the cement floor covered with graphite dust was slippery.'

Fermi's calculations

Guiding the design and construction of the pile construction was Fermi, who was described by his associates as 'completely self-confident but wholly without conceit'. So precise were Fermi's calculations that days before its completion, he was able to predict almost to the exact brick the point at which the reactor would become self-sustaining.

Even though the pile had not even been completed and tested yet, a lot was riding on it. In Washington, MED had commissioned DuPont to design, build and operate a plant based on the principles of the Chicago pile – if it proved a success. The result was the $350-million Hanford Engineer Works at Pasco, Washington.

In Chicago in the early afternoon of 1 December, tests indicated that the pile was reaching critical size. At that point Fermi's massive lattice pile contained some 400 tons of graphite, 6 tons of uranium metal and 50 tons of uranium oxide.

At 4pm, Zinn's group was relieved by the men working under Anderson. Shortly afterwards, the last layer of graphite and uranium bricks was placed on the pile. Zinn and Anderson made several measurements of the activity within the pile. They were certain that when the cadmium rods that absorbed neutrons and controlled the reaction were withdrawn, the activity in the pile would become self-sustaining. But they agreed that they would not start the pile operating until Fermi and the rest of the group were present. So the control rods were locked in position and further work was postponed until the following day.

The first test

About 8.30am on the morning of Wednesday, 2 December, the scientists began to assemble at the squash court where the pile had been built. At the north end of the court was a balcony about 10 feet above the floor of the court. Fermi, Zinn, Anderson and Compton were grouped around instruments at the east end of the balcony. The remainder of the observers crowded into the rest of the little gallery. One of the young scientists who worked on the pile said: 'The control cabinet was surrounded by the "big wheels"; the "little wheels" had to stand back.' On the floor of the squash court, just beneath the balcony, stood George Weil, who had been with Fermi at Columbia. His duty was to handle the final control rod.

Enrico Fermi directs a large Goodyear balloon to hang over his Chicago Pile 1, the first nuclear chain reactor. The pile was built in the doubles squash court in the west stands of the University of Chicago's Stagg Field. Fermi and other scientists watch from the balcony of the squash court.

In the pile were four control rods. These were made of cadmium that was capable of absorbing neutrons without fissioning itself. One was operated by small electric motors and could be controlled from the balcony. Another was a safety rod, called 'Zip'. This was activated by a solenoid. If the neutron intensity exceeded a predetermined setting, the solenoid would trip and the weighted rod would drop into place under the force of gravity.

There was also an emergency rod, to be withdrawn from the pile by hand and hung by a rope from the balcony. If anything went wrong and the automatic safety rod failed, Hilberry was to cut this rope with an axe. Again the rod would fall into place in the pile, closing down the reaction. The fourth control rod, operated by hand by Weil, was the one that actually controlled the reaction.

As nothing like this had been done before, safety was

paramount, so it was decided that complete reliance would not be placed on mechanical control rods. A three-man 'liquid-control squad' mustered on a platform above the pile. This suicide team was ready to douse the pile with cadmium-sulphate solution in case of mechanical failure of the control rods. This again would close down the reaction.

Rods out

Each group rehearsed its part of the experiment. Then at 9.45am, Fermi ordered the electrically operated control rods withdrawn. The man at the controls threw the switch and a small motor whined. All eyes watched the lights that indicated the rods' position.

Quickly, the balcony group turned to watch the neutron counters, whose clicking stepped up after the rods were out. The indicators of these counters resembled the face of a clock. Nearby was a cylindrical pen recorder, whose quivering stylus traced the neutron activity within the pile. Meanwhile, Fermi clutched a slide rule to do rapid calculations.

Shortly after 10am, Fermi ordered the emergency rod to be pulled out. Weil stood ready by the 'vernier' control rod, which was marked to show the length that remained within the pile.

At 10.37am, without taking his eyes off the instruments, Fermi said quietly: 'Pull it to 13 feet, George.'

As Weil edged the rod halfway out, the counters clicked faster. The graph pen moved up. The instruments were studied and computations made.

'This is not it,' said Fermi. 'The trace will go to this point and level off.'

Slowly the pen rose to the point he indicated, but did not move any higher. Seven minutes later Fermi ordered Weil to pull the rod out another foot. Again the graph pen edged upwards and the counters stepped up their clicking. But the clicking was irregular and the line made by the pen levelled off. The reaction in the pile was not self-sustaining – yet.

At 11am, the rod was withdrawn another 6 inches. The result was the same. The rate increased, then levelled off.

Fifteen minutes later, the rod was withdrawn further and at 11.25am was edged out again. Each time the clicking of the counters speeded up and the pen rose a few points. Fermi predicted every movement of the indicators correctly. He knew that the pile was nearly going critical, but he wanted to check everything once again. So the automatic control rod was reinserted. The graph line dropped and the counters slowed.

At 11.35am, the automatic safety rod was withdrawn again. Up went the counters, clicking, clicking, faster and faster, and the graph pen started to climb. Tensely, the little group watched entranced.

Then there was a loud crash. The spectators froze – then breathed a sigh of relief. The thunder-clap was the sound of the automatic safety rod slamming home. The point where the rod operated automatically had been set too low, so it had fallen back into place.

'I'm hungry,' said Fermi. 'Let's go to lunch.'

Self-sustaining

Over lunch the team talked of everything else but the test. The habitually taciturn Fermi was even more close-lipped than usual. At 2pm, they trooped back to the squash court. Twenty minutes later, the automatic rod had been reset and Weil stood ready at the control rod.

'All right, George,' said Fermi and Weil pulled the rod out.

At 2.50pm he withdrew it another foot. The counters nearly jammed and the pen headed off the graph paper. But this was not it. Counting ratios and the graph scale had to be changed.

At 3.20pm Fermi told Weil: 'Move it six inches.'

Again the levels rose, but again levelled off.

Five minutes later, Fermi said: 'Pull it out another foot.'

Weil obliged.

'This is going to do it,' Fermi said to Compton. 'Now it will become self-sustaining. The trace will climb and continue to climb. It will not level off.'

Fermi computed the rate of rise of the neutron counts over the period of a minute. Silently, he ran through the calculations on his slide rule.

About a minute later, he computed the rate of rise again. If the rate remained constant, he would know the reaction was self-sustaining. Three minutes later he computed the rate of rise in neutron count yet again. By then the clicking of the counters was a constant buzz.

'I couldn't see the instruments,' said Weil. 'I had to watch Fermi every second, waiting for orders. He face was motion-less. His eyes darted from one dial to another. His expression was so calm it was hard to read. But suddenly, his whole face broke into a broad smile.'

Then Fermi closed his slide rule.

'The reaction is self-sustaining,' he announced quietly, happily. 'The curve is exponential.'

Closing down

The world's first nuclear chain reactor operated for 28 minutes. At 3.53pm, the control rods were replaced. The counters slowed and the pen headed downwards across the paper. The test was over. The team had succeeded in initiating a self-sustaining nuclear reaction – and then stopping it. They had released the energy of the atom's nucleus and controlled it.

Once the pile was closed down, Wigner presented Fermi with a flask of Chianti, which he had kept hidden behind his back throughout the experiment. He had been saving it for the occasion; with the US at war with Italy, no Italian wine could be imported.

Fermi sent out for paper cups and uncorked the bottle. He poured a little wine in all the cups and solemnly, without a toast, they raised the cups to their lips and drank silently to success – and to the hope they had been the first to succeed. Afterwards, Fermi and the others signed the straw wrapping on the bottle.

Compton then phoned Conant at Harvard and delivered a message in the pre-arranged code.

'Jim,' said Compton. 'The Italian navigator has landed in the New World.'

'Is that so,' said Conant. 'How were the natives?'

'Everyone landed safe and happy,' Compton replied.

As the crew filed out of the West Stands, one of the guards asked Zinn: 'What's going on, Doctor, something happen in there?'

On this momentous day in scientific history, they had generated half a watt of energy. That would be increased to 200 watts 10 days later – enough to power two light bulbs.

Presidential approval

DuPoint's Crawford H. Greenewalt, a member of the Lewis Committee, had been present at Stagg Field on 2 December. A week later, the S-1 Executive Committee met to consider the Lewis Committee's report. Most of the morning session was spent evaluating the controversial recommendation that only a small electromagnetic separation plant be built. Lewis and his colleagues based their recommendation on the belief that Lawrence could not produce enough U-235 to be of military significance. However, since the calutron could provide enriched samples quickly, it was worth taking forward to a limited extent.

Conant disagreed with the Lewis Committee's assessment, believing that uranium had more weapons potential than plutonium. And since he knew that gaseous diffusion could not provide any enriched uranium until a large gaseous diffusion plant was in full operation, he supported electromagnetic separation as the one method that might, if all went well, produce enough uranium to build a bomb in 1944.

During the afternoon, the S-1 Executive Committee went over a draft that Groves had prepared for Bush to send to the president. It supported the Lewis Committee's report, except that it recommended skipping the pilot plant stage for the pile. Conant and the Lewis Committee met again the following day and reached a compromise on the electro-magnetic method. Groves's draft was then amended and forwarded to Bush.

On 28 December 1942, President Roosevelt approved the spending of $500 million as itemized in Bush's report. In the end, the government would spend over $2 billion on the bomb.

With the president's signature, the Manhattan Project was authorized to build full-scale gaseous diffusion and plutonium plants and a scaled-down electromagnetic plant, as well as heavy water production facilities. In his report, Bush reaffirmed his belief that it might be possible to built a bomb in the first half of 1945 – though delivery earlier than that was unlikely. He also warned that no schedule could guarantee that the US could overtake Germany in the race for the bomb.

Nevertheless, by the beginning of 1943, the Manhattan Project had the complete support of President Roosevelt and the military leadership, and the services of some of the world's most distinguished scientists.

Chapter Five
The Biggest Secret

In many ways, the Manhattan Engineer District operated like any other large construction company. It purchased and prepared sites, issued contracts, hired personnel and subcontractors, built and maintained housing and service facilities, placed orders for materials, developed administrative and accounting procedures, and established communications networks. By the end of the war, Groves and his staff had spent approximately $2.2 billion on production facilities, building towns in Tennessee, Washington and New Mexico, and conducting research in university laboratories from Columbia to Berkeley. What made the Manhattan Project unlike other enterprises was that, because it had to move quickly, it invested hundreds of millions of dollars in unproven and hitherto unknown processes – and everything it did had to be done in secret.

Secrecy meant that its operations had to be undertaken in remote locations. Subterfuge was required in obtaining labour and supplies. This became a constant irritant to the academic scientists on the project – men who were used to having open discussions and publishing their findings. Indeed, secrecy was so complete that many people employed did not know what they were working on until they heard about the bombing of Hiroshima on the radio.

However, secrecy had one overwhelming advantage. It made it possible to take decisions without regard for normal peacetime political considerations. Groves knew that as long as he had the backing of the White House, money would be available. There could be no intervention by Congress, and he would not be answerable to the press or public opinion. He could devote his considerable energies entirely to running the bomb project.

The scale, too, was breathtaking. Bertrand Goldschmidt, a French chemist who worked alongside Seaborg, said: 'The astonishing American creation in three years, at a cost of two billion dollars, of a formidable array of factories and laboratories was as large as the entire automobile industry of the United States at that date.'

The need for haste clarified priorities and shaped decision-making. Unfinished research on three separate, unproven processes had to be used to draw up design plans for production facilities, even though later findings inevitably would dictate changes.

Normally, when taking a scientific process into production, a pilot plant would be built. This stage was eliminated entirely, violating all manufacturing practices. It led to intermittent shutdowns and endless troubleshooting during trial runs in production facilities, and cycles of optimism and despair.

Despite Bush's assertion that a bomb could probably be produced by 1945, he knew it would be no easy task. For any large organization to take laboratory research through the design, construction and operation of a manufacturing facility up to the delivery of a product in two-and-a-half years would be a major achievement. Whether the Manhattan Project would be able to produce bombs in time to affect the current conflict was an open question as 1943 began.

Plainly, no one knew then how long the war would last. In

January 1943, US troops were still stuck on Guadalcanal. The Germans were still fighting in North Africa. They had yet to be turned back at Stalingrad, and there been no Anglo-American landings on the Continent. Although the tide appeared to be turning, the end of the war still seemed a long, long way away.

Oak Ridge

By the time President Roosevelt authorized the Manhattan Project on 28 December 1942, work on the east Tennessee site where the first production facilities were to be built was already underway. Some 90 square miles of land had been bought in the ridges just west of Knoxville. The relatively few families living on the marginal farmland were to be removed and the site had to be prepared. Transportation, communications and utilities had to be provided for the production plants and the workforce, and around 13,000 people would need accommodation in prefabricated housing, trailers and wooden dormitories. This military reservation would be called the Clinton Engineer Works, later to become known as Oak Ridge.

Groves kept the Manhattan Project's office in Washington, but put the Manhattan Engineer District headquarters in Tennessee under the command of Nichols in the summer of 1943. By then, estimates for the population of the town of Oak Ridge had been revised upwards to 40,000–45,000 people. While the army and its contractors tried to keep up with the rapid influx of workers and their families, services always lagged behind demand. Nevertheless, morale remained high in what was essentially an atomic boom-town. By the end of the war, Oak Ridge would be the fifth largest town in Tennessee, and the Clinton Engineer Works would

X-10 at Oak Ridge National Laboratory in Tennessee.

be consuming one-seventh of all the power produced
in America.

The three production facility sites were located in valleys
away from the town. This made security easier and the
ridges provided containment in case of accidents. The Y-12
area, home of the electromagnetic plant, was closest to Oak
Ridge, just one valley to the south. Farther to the south and
west lay both the X-10 area, which contained the experimental plutonium pile and separation facilities, and K-25, the
site of the gaseous diffusion plant and later the S-50 thermal
diffusion plant. Y-12 and X-10 were begun slightly earlier in
1943 than K-25, but all three were well along by the end
of the year.

The design of Y-12 electromagnetic plant

Although the Lewis report had placed gaseous diffusion ahead of the electromagnetic method of separation, in early 1943 many were still betting that Lawrence and his mass spectrograph would eventually win the race. While building was underway, Lawrence and collaborators at Berkeley continued to experiment with the giant 184-inch magnet, trying to finalize the design for the Oak Ridge plant. Research on magnet size and placement and beam resolution eventually led to a racetrack configuration of two magnets with 48 gaps containing two vacuum tanks each per building. Ten buildings would be necessary to provide the 2000 sources and collectors needed to separate 100 grams of U-235 a day. It was hoped that improvements in calutron design, or placing multiple sources and collectors in each tank, might increase efficiency and reduce the number of tanks and buildings required, but experimental results were inconclusive even as the contractor Stone & Webster of Boston prepared to break ground for the Y-12 facility at Oak Ridge.

At a meeting between Groves, Lawrence and John R. Lotz of Stone & Webster in Berkeley late in December 1942, the plans for Y-12 had already taken shape. It was agreed that Stone & Webster would take over design and construction of a 500-tank facility, while Lawrence's laboratory would play a supporting role by supplying experimental data.

By the time another summit conference on Y-12 took place in Berkeley on 13 January 1943, Groves had persuaded the Tennessee Eastman Corporation to sign on as plant operator and arranged for various parts of the electromagnetic equipment to be manufactured by the Westinghouse Electric and Manufacturing Company, the Allis-Chalmers Manufacturing Company and the Chapman Valve Manufacturing Company. General Electric agreed to provide the electrics.

On 14 January, after a day of presentations and a demonstration of the experimental tanks in the cyclotron building, Groves insisted that the Y-12 contractors have the first racetrack of 96 tanks in operation by 1 July and that 500 tanks be delivered by the year's end. Each racetrack was to be 122 feet long, 77 feet wide and 15 feet high, and the completed plant would be the size of three two-storey buildings. Meanwhile, tank design was still being modified and chemical extraction facilities also would have to be built. Nevertheless, Groves maintained that his schedule could be met.

For the next two months, Lawrence, the contractors and the army argued over the final design. While everyone involved could see possible improvements, there was not enough time to incorporate every suggested modification. Y-12 design was finalized at a meeting in Boston on 17 March with one major modification – the inclusion of a second stage of the electromagnetic process.

This second stage would take the enriched U-235 produced by several runs of the first stage and use it as feed for secondary racetracks, which contained tanks approximately half the size of those in the first. Groves approved this arrangement and work began on both the Alpha (first-stage) and Beta (second-stage) tracks.

The construction of Y-12

Ground-breaking for the Alpha plant took place on 18 February 1943. Soon blueprints could not be produced fast enough to keep up with construction as Stone & Webster struggled to meet Groves's deadline; the Beta facility was actually begun before formal authorization. The project was dogged by a shortage of workers skilled enough to perform jobs to the rigid specifications and this was further

Alpha Track, Y-12 plant, Oak Ridge National Laboratory.

complicated as some tasks could be performed only by workers with special clearance.

Huge amounts of material had to be obtained. More than three million cubic feet of board timber were required, for instance, and the magnets needed so much copper for windings that the Army had to substitute silver, borrowing almost 15,000 tons of silver bullion from the US Treasury. Treasury silver was also used to manufacture the bus bars that carried the high electrical currents needed around the top of the racetracks.

Replacing copper with silver solved the immediate problem of the magnets and bus bars, but persistent shortages of vacuum tubes, generators, regulators and other equipment posed a serious threat to Groves's deadline. Furthermore, last-minute design changes continued to frustrate equipment manufacturers. Nevertheless, when Lawrence toured with Y-12 contractors in May 1943, he was impressed by the scale of operations.

Design changes at Y-12

Back at Berkeley, Lawrence and his colleagues continued to look for ways to improve the electromagnetic process. Lawrence found that hot – high positive voltage – electrical sources could replace the single cold, grounded source in future plants, providing more efficient use of power, reducing insulator failure and making it possible to use multiple rather than single beams. Meanwhile, design of the receivers

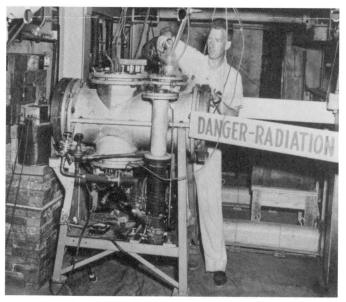

A technician at Oak Ridge.

collecting the U-235 evolved quickly enough in spring and summer 1943 to be incorporated into the Alpha plant. Work at the Radiation Laboratory picked up more speed in March with the authorization of the Beta process, planning a second stage of the electromagnetic process that had not been anticipated.

While the scientists in Berkeley studied changes that would be required in the smaller Beta racetracks, engineering work at Oak Ridge also generated design modifications. For a number of reasons, including the simplicity of maintenance, Tennessee Eastman decided that the Beta plant would consist of a rectangular – rather than oval – arrangement of two tracks of 36 tanks each.

Factoring this configuration into their calculations, Lawrence and his co-workers bent their efforts to developing chemical processing techniques that would minimize the loss of enriched uranium during Beta production runs. To make certain that Alpha had enough feed material, Lawrence arranged for research on an alternate method at Brown University and expanded efforts at Berkeley. With what was left of his time and money, in early 1943, Lawrence built prototypes of Alpha and Beta units for testing and training operating personnel. Meanwhile Tennessee Eastman, running behind schedule, raced to complete experimental models so that training and test runs could be performed at Oak Ridge.

While progress was being made in construction, and research on the electromagnetic process was progressing, discouraging news came from Oppenheimer's isolated laboratory in Los Alamos, New Mexico, in July.

Los Alamos

While Bush was seeking approval from the president, Oppenheimer had suggested that a bomb laboratory be set up

The Trailer Housing Area at Los Alamos.

in an isolated area. It would operate secretly but allow a free exchange of ideas between theoreticians and experimentalists who would work side by side.

The search for a bomb laboratory site quickly narrowed to two places in northern New Mexico – Jemez Springs and the Los Alamos Boys Ranch School. Oppenheimer knew these two locations well as he had a ranch nearby in the Pecos Valley of the Sangre de Cristo Mountains. In mid-November, Oppenheimer, Groves, McMillan and Lieutenant Colonel W. H. Dudley visited the two sites and chose Los Alamos; though it was easy enough to get to Santa Fe by train, Los Alamos itself was virtually inaccessible, located on a mesa, or flat-topped hill, about 30 miles northwest. It would have to be provided with better water and power facilities, but the laboratory community was not expected to be very large. The owners of the boys' school occupying the site were eager to sell, and Groves was equally eager to buy. By the end of 1942 the district engineer in Albuquerque had orders to begin construction, and the University of California had contracted to provide supplies and personnel.

Groves and Oppenheimer were as different as chalk and cheese. A practical-minded military man, Groves was brusque and goal-oriented. He demanded that the Manhattan Project scientists spend all their time on the bomb and resist the temptation, harmless enough in peacetime, to follow lines of research that had no direct applicability to immediate problems. In contrast, Oppenheimer was a philosophical man, attracted to Eastern mysticism. He was of a decidedly theoretical inclination and sensitive nature.

Oppenheimer was picked to head the new laboratory, despite initial concerns about his administrative inexperience, leftist political sympathies and lack of a Nobel Prize when several scientists who would be working under him were prize-winners. A chain-smoker given to long working hours, he appeared almost emaciated compared to the rotund Groves. Nevertheless, the Groves-Oppenheimer alliance, though not one of intimacy, was marked by mutual respect and was a major factor in the success of the Manhattan Project.

Oppenheimer insisted, with some success, that the group of scientists at Los Alamos should be as much an academic community as possible, and he proved adept at satisfying the emotional and intellectual needs of his highly distinguished staff. Hans Bethe, head of the theoretical division, remembered that nobody else in that laboratory 'even came close to him in his knowledge. There was human warmth as well. Everybody certainly had the impression that Oppenheimer cared what each particular person was doing. In talking to someone he made it clear that that person's work was important for the success of the whole project.'

While Groves's visits were always an interruption, Bethe remembered the day Oppenheimer dropped into a session where an inconclusive debate over what type of refractory container should be used for melting plutonium was going on. After listening to the argument, Oppenheimer summed up the discussion. He did not directly propose a solution, but by the time he left the room, the right answer was clear to everyone.

'Oppenheimer insisted that everybody at the Los Alamos Laboratory could know everything,' said Bethe. 'More than that, he insisted that the group leaders and senior scientists come to weekly meetings in which absolutely everything was discussed in detail. Scientists did that with enthusiasm. Oppenheimer thereby created a spirit of the lab as a whole that was one of his great contributions.'

Oppenheimer displayed his persuasive abilities early on when he had to convince scientists, many of them already deeply involved in war-related research in university laboratories, to join his new organization. This was made more difficult due to early plans to operate Los Alamos as a military establishment. Oppenheimer accepted Groves's rationale for this arrangement but soon found that scientists objected to working as commissioned officers and feared that the military chain of command was ill-suited to making decisions on scientific matters.

The issue came to a head when Oppenheimer tried to convince Robert F. Bacher and Isidor I. Rabi of the MIT's Radiation Laboratory to join the Los Alamos team. Neither thought a military environment was conducive to scientific research. At Oppenheimer's request, Conant and Groves wrote a letter explaining that the secret weapon-related research had presidential authority and was of the utmost national importance. The letter promised that the laboratory would remain civilian through 1943, when it was believed that the requirements of security would require militarization of the final stages of the project – though, in fact, militarization never took place. Oppenheimer would supervise all scientific work, and the military would be limited to providing security and maintaining the post.

Bad news from New Mexico

Once work was underway at Los Alamos, Oppenheimer discovered that three times more fissionable material would be required for a bomb than earlier estimates had indicated. Even with satisfactory performance of the racetracks at Oak Ridge, it was possible that they might not produce enough purified U-235 in time.

Lawrence responded to this crisis in characteristic fashion. He immediately lobbied Groves to incorporate multiple sources into the racetracks already under construction and build more racetracks. Groves decided to build the first four racetracks as planned then, after receiving favourable reports from both Stone & Webster and Tennessee Eastman, allowed a four-beam source to be incorporated in the fifth.

Convinced that the electromagnetic process would work and sensing that estimates from Los Alamos might be revised downward in the future, Groves let Lawrence talk him into building a new plant – in effect, doubling the size of the electromagnetic complex. Groves reported to the Military Policy Committee on 9 September 1943 that the new facility would consist of two buildings, each with two rectangular racetracks of 96 tanks operating with four-beam sources.

Shakedown at Y-12

In the summer and autumn of 1943 the first electromagnetic plant began to take shape. The huge building housing the operating equipment was prepared as manufacturers began delivering electrical switches, motors, valves and tanks. While construction and outfitting proceeded, nearly 5000 operating and maintenance personnel were hired and trained. Then, between October and mid-December, everything began to go wrong. Vacuum tanks in the first Alpha racetrack leaked. The intense magnetic field pushed them out of line and welds cracked. Circuits failed and operators made mistakes. Most seriously, the magnet coils shorted out because of rust and sediment in the cooling oil.

When Groves arrived on 15 December 1943, he shut the racetrack down. The coils were sent to Allis-Chalmers with hope that they could be cleaned without being dismantled entirely, while other measures were taken to prevent a recurrence of the shorting.

Effort switched to the second Alpha, but it fared little better when it started up in mid-January 1944. While all the tanks operated for short periods, its performance was sporadic and there were frequent electrical failures and breakdowns due to defective parts. It was another maintenance nightmare.

Nevertheless, Alpha 2 produced about 200 grams of 12 per cent U-235 by the end of February, enough to send samples to Los Alamos and feed the first Beta unit. The first four Alpha tracks did not operate together until April, four months behind schedule. While maintenance improved, output still fell far short of expectations. The opening of the Beta building on 11 March was also a disappointment; beam resolution was so poor that a complete redesign was needed.

Gaseous diffusion problems

While electromagnetic separation was having difficulties, the K-25 gaseous diffusion process was also in deep trouble because of the continuing problem of finding a practical barrier. Championed by the British, gaseous diffusion seemed to be based on sound theory. It had been made number-one priority by the Lewis Committee, though it had not yet

The solution of the K-25 site forced the Jones Construction Company to build housing facilities for workers. The Jones camp, which was nicknamed 'Happy Valley' by its inhabitants, eventually had a total population of about 15,000.

produced a single sample of enriched U-235. Nevertheless, the full-scale project had been given the go-ahead.

Preparation for the K-25 power plant began in June at a site on a relatively flat area of about 5000 acres southwest of Oak Ridge on the Clinch River. Throughout the summer, contractors shipped in the materials needed to build what became the world's largest steam electric plant over the primitive roads. In September, work began on the cascade building, plans for which had changed dramatically since the spring. Now there were to be 50 four-storey buildings in a U-shape, measuring half a mile by 1000 feet. They would cover 2,000,000 square feet and, to cut the time needed to set thousands of concrete piers to support load-bearing walls, new techniques of building foundations were developed.

As it was 11 miles from the headquarters at Oak Ridge, the K-25 site developed into a satellite town. Housing and a full array of service facilities had to be laid on for a population that reached 15,000. Dubbed 'Happy Valley' by the inhabitants, the town had housing similar to that in Oak Ridge. It too experienced chronic shortages. Even using the contractor camp with facilities for 2000 employees nearby, half of Happy Valley's workers had to commute to the construction site daily. K-25 had been counted upon to provide uranium enriched enough to serve as feed material for the Beta racetracks. Now it would be producing such slight enrichment that the Alpha tracks would have to process K-25's material, requiring extensive redesign and retooling.

To process the slightly enriched material produced by K-25, Groves set to work on a further expansion of the electromagnetic facilities. Lawrence, seconded by Oppenheimer, believed that four more racetracks should be built to accompany the nine already finished or under construction. Groves agreed, though he was not sure that the additional racetracks could be built in time.

As the prospects of using plutonium remained uncertain, Lawrence came up with a plan to convert all tanks to multiple beams and to build two more racetracks. By this time the British had given up on gaseous diffusion and urged acceptance of Lawrence's plan.

At a meeting on 4 July 1944, Groves and the Oak Ridge contractors considered the proposals Lawrence had made. They decided that there was not enough time to change the completed racetracks; instead, some improvements should be made in the racetracks then under construction. The most important decision made at the meeting was that Lawrence should throw everything he had into a completely new type of calutron that would use a 30-beam source. Technical support would come from both Westinghouse and General Electric, who would stop work on four-beam development. This was a risky gamble in a high-stakes game.

Downgrading K-25

In the late summer of 1943 it was decided that K-25 would play a lesser role than originally intended. Instead of producing fully enriched U-235, the gaseous diffusion plant would now provide around 50 per cent enrichment for use as feed material in Y-12. This would allow the more troublesome upper part of the cascade to be eliminated. Even this level of enrichment was not assured, since a barrier suitable for the diffusion plant had still not been found. The downgrading of K-25 was part of the larger decision to double Y-12 capacity as part of Groves's new strategy of using a combination of methods to produce enough fissionable material for bombs as soon as possible.

Groves was still convinced that gaseous diffusion had to be pursued vigorously. Not only had major resources been expended on the programme, there was still a possibility that it might yet prove successful. The electromagnetic method could not be relied on as Y-12 was in trouble as 1944 began, and the plutonium pile projects were only just getting underway. If the scientists came up with a workable barrier design, it might put K-25 ahead in the race for the bomb. So Groves ordered a crash barrier programme, hoping to prevent K-25 from standing idle as the race for the bomb continued.

Help from the navy

While the Manhattan Project had been given to the army, the navy had been researching atomic power independently, primarily for use in submarines. In April 1944, Oppenheimer wrote to Groves, telling him that Philip Abelson's experiments on thermal diffusion at the Philadelphia Naval Yard deserved a closer look. Abelson was building a plant to produce enriched uranium due to be completed in early July. If Groves helped Abelson complete and expand his plant, Oppenheimer thought it might be possible to use its slightly enriched product as feed for Y-12 until problems with K-25 could be overcome.

The liquid thermal diffusion process had been evaluated in 1940 by the Uranium Committee and dismissed. Abelson had then been at the National Bureau of Standards. The following year he moved to the Naval Research Laboratory, where there was more support for his work.

During the summer of 1942 Bush and Conant had received reports about Abelson's research, but decided that it would take too long for the thermal diffusion process to make a major contribution to the bomb effort. Besides, at the time, the electromagnetic and pile projects were making satisfactory progress.

After visiting with Abelson in January 1943, Bush encouraged the navy to increase its support of thermal diffusion. A thorough review of Abelson's project early in 1943 concluded that work on thermal diffusion should be expanded, but it should not be considered as a replacement for gaseous diffusion which was better understood theoretically. While Abelson continued his work independently of the Manhattan Project, he obtained authorization to build a new plant at the Philadelphia Naval Yard. Construction began there in January 1944.

After receiving Oppenheimer's letter, Groves immediately sent a group to Philadelphia to inspect Abelson's plant. They quickly concluded that a thermal diffusion plant could be built at Oak Ridge and be in operation by early 1945. The steam needed in the convection columns could be obtained from the K-25 power plant which was nearing completion. While Abelson's navy-yard plant had just 100 columns, on 27 September Groves gave the contractor, H. K. Ferguson Company of Cleveland, just 90 days to get a 2142-column plant up and running, and Happy Valley braced itself for a huge new influx of workers.

Chapter Six

Plutonium Piles

Work had been underway at the Metallurgical Laboratory in Chicago to design a production pile to produce plutonium. Again the job was to design equipment for a technology that was not well understood even in the laboratory. The Fermi pile, important as it was historically, provided little technical guidance other than to suggest a lattice arrangement of graphite and uranium. Any pile producing more power than the few watts generated in Fermi's early experiments would require elaborate controls, radiation shielding and a cooling system. These engineering features would all cause a reduction in neutron multiplication, k. So the problem was to design a pile that would be safe and controllable, while still having a k high enough to sustain an on-going reaction.

A group headed by Compton's chief engineer, Thomas V. Moore, began designing the production pile in June 1942. Its first goals were to find the best methods of extracting plutonium from the irradiated uranium and for cooling the uranium, which became dangerously hot when a chain reaction was underway. It quickly became clear that a production pile would differ significantly in design from Fermi's experimental reactor, possibly by extending uranium rods into and through the graphite next to cooling tubes. A radiation and containment shield would also need to be built.

Cooling

Although experimental reactors like Fermi's did not generate enough power to need cooling systems, piles built to produce plutonium would operate at high power levels and require coolants. The Met Lab group considered the full range of gases and liquids. Among the gases, hydrogen and helium were the best candidates; water was the best liquid, even though it has a tendency to corrode uranium.

During the summer, Moore and his group began planning a helium-cooled pilot pile built by Stone & Webster on the Argonne Forest Preserve near Chicago. On 25 September they submitted their proposal to Compton. The pile would be a 460-ton cube of graphite to be pierced by 376 vertical columns containing 22 cartridges of uranium and graphite. Cooling would be provided by circulating helium through the pile. A wall of graphite surrounding the reactor would provide radiation containment, while the outer shell would comprise a series of spherical segments that gave the design the nickname 'Mae West'.

By the time Compton received Moore's report, he had two other pile designs to consider. One was a water-cooled model developed by Eugene Wigner and Gale Young, a former colleague of Compton's. Wigner and Young proposed a 12 x 25 foot cylinder of graphite with pipes of uranium extending from a water tank above, through the cylinder, and into a second water tank underneath. Coolant would circulate continuously through the system, and corrosion would be minimized by coating interior surfaces or lining the uranium pipes.

The Hungarian-American physicist Leo Szilard (1898-1964).

A second alternative was more daring. Szilard thought that liquid metal would be a very efficient coolant. Circulated by an electromagnetic pump having no moving parts, adapted from a design he and Einstein had patented, it would be possible to achieve high power levels in a considerably smaller pile. The problem was that bismuth, the metal he favoured as the coolant, was rare.

Groves steps in

Compton could not make up his mind. He favoured the helium-cooled Mae West design, but engineering studies could not go ahead until the precise value of k had been established. Some scientists at the Met Lab urged that a full production pile be built immediately, while others advocated a multi-step process, perhaps beginning with an externally cooled reactor proposed by Fermi. The situation was resolved when Groves arrived in Chicago.

On 5 October 1942, Groves told Met Lab to make a decision on pile design within a week. Even wrong decisions were better than no decisions, Groves said. And as time was more valuable than money, more than one approach should be pursued if no single design stood out.

That was the route Compton decided to take. Fermi would work on a small experimental unit to be completed and in operation by the end of the year. This would allow him to determine the precise value of k and render significant advances in pile engineering. An intermediate pile with external cooling would be built at Argonne and operated until 1 June 1943, when it would be taken down so the plutonium could be extracted. The helium-cooled Mae West, designed to produce 100 grams of plutonium a day, would be built and in operation by March 1944. Meanwhile, studies on liquid-cooled reactors would continue, including Szilard's work on the use of liquid metals.

Plutonium chemistry

While decisions were being made on pile design, Glenn Seaborg and his team tried to gain enough information about transuranium chemistry to insure that the plutonium produced could be successfully extracted from the irradiated uranium. They worked on a uranium compound that had been bombarded in a cyclotron, handling the radioactive material with just rubber gloves and lab coats for protection.

Three hundred pounds of the yellowish, crystalline material uranyl nitrate hexahydrate (UNH) was brought in by truck from St Louis. Some of the plywood boxes had split open, allowing crystals of hot, radioactive UNH to spill out. During the chemical separation, the researchers wrestled carboys of ether and 3-litre separation funnels held at arm's length from behind lead shields.

The chemical process was complex, but on 20 August 1942, Seaborg wrote: 'Perhaps today was the most exciting and thrilling day I have experienced since coming to the Met Lab. Our microchemists isolated pure element 94 for the first time! . . . This precipitate of 94, which was viewed under the microscope and which was also visible to the naked eye, did not differ visibly from the rare-earth florides . . . It is the first time that element 94 . . . has been beheld by the eye of man.'

It was pinkish in colour. Seaborg and team had to perform ultramicrochemistry on quantities so small they were measured in tenths of a microgram. By comparison, a British penny weighs 3.56 grams or 3,560,000 micrograms; an American dime weighs 2,268 grams or 2,268,000 micrograms.

Work would have to be done under a binocular stereo-
scopic microscope with x30 magnification. Fine glass capillary straws were used instead of test tubs and beakers. These
filled automatically by capillary action. To weigh a sample, a
single fibre of quartz was fixed at one end like a fishing rod
stuck in a riverbank. A weighing pan was made of a snippet
of platinum foil, itself almost too small to see. This was
attached to the free end of the quartz fibre and the weight
was measured by how much the fibre deflected. All this had
to be done within a glass housing to protect it from the least
breath of air. At Berkeley, the team suspended double pans
from the opposite ends of a quartz-fibre beam on microscopic
struts. Seaborg noted that it was as if 'invisible material was
being weighed on an invisible balance'.

Seaborg's discovery and subsequent isolation of plutonium
were major events in the history of chemistry but, like Fermi's
achievement in making an atomic pile, it remained to be seen
whether they could be translated into a production process
that would help to make an atomic bomb. In fact, the challenge
of Seaborg's work seemed even more daunting. While piles had
to be scaled up just 10 or 20 times, a separation plant for
plutonium would involve a scale-up of the laboratory experiment on the order of a billion-fold.

Collaboration with DuPont's Charles M. Cooper and his staff
on plutonium separation facilities had began even before
Seaborg succeeded in isolating the first sample of plutonium.
Seaborg's method involved the chemical lanthanum fluoride.
But three other methods of separation were under
consideration. Seaborg and Cooper decided to pursue all four
methods of plutonium separation, though first priority was the
lanthanum-fluoride process Seaborg had already succeeded
with. Cooper's staff ran into problems with the lanthanum
fluoride method in late 1942. By then Seaborg had become
interested in work led by Stanley G. Thompson using bismuth

phosphate. With bismuth phosphate as a backup for the lanthanum fluoride process, Cooper moved ahead on a pilot plant near Stagg Field.

Safety first

While Compton had originally planned to build a small experimental pile and chemical separation plant on the University of Chicago campus, in the autumn of 1942, the S-1 Executive Committee agreed that it would be safer to put Fermi's pile at Argonne and build the pilot plant and separation facilities in Oak Ridge, rather than undertake these experiments in a populous area.

On 3 October DuPont agreed to design and build the chemical separation plant. Groves tried to entice DuPont into further participation at Oak Ridge by having the firm prepare an appraisal of the pile project and by placing three DuPont staff members on the Lewis Committee. The company was reluctant to participate as it was still smarting from charges of profiteering in World War I, but Groves eventually secured the services of the chemical giant for one dollar over costs. DuPont was so sensitive about its public image that it vowed to stay out of the bomb business after the war and offered all the patents it secured to the US government.

The company became a vital addition to the bomb project because of its well-established administrative structure. Nevertheless, it proceeded with caution. After studying every aspect of the Met Lab's programme, it insisted on being put in full charge of the Oak Ridge plutonium project. It was then decided that there was not room for a full-scale separation plant at the X-10 site, nor was there the generating power needed for yet another major facility. Furthermore, the site was uncomfortably close to Knoxville should a catastrophe

The X-10 Graphite Reactor supplied the Los Alamos laboratory with the first significant amounts of plutonium.

occur. So the search began for an alternate site for the full-scale plutonium facility. Compton's scientists estimated they needed an area of around 225 square miles. There would be three or four piles and one or two chemical separation complexes. The piles would have to be at least a mile apart for security purposes, while nothing would be allowed within 4 miles of the separation complexes for fear of radioactive accidents. Towns, laboratories, highways and rail lines would all have to be several miles further away.

Hanford

December 1942 found Colonel Franklin T. Matthias from Groves's staff and two DuPont engineers heading for the Pacific Northwest and southern California to investigate possible production sites. They were looking for large, isolated sites where there would be a long construction season. Along the Columbia and Colorado Rivers there was the added bonus of abundant hydroelectric power.

One of the three pile areas at the Hanford Engineer Works. These are the manufacturing areas where plutonium is made.

After viewing six sites in Washington, Oregon and California, the group agreed that the area around Hanford, Washington, best met the criteria established by the Met Lab scientists and DuPont engineers. The Grand Coulee and Bonneville dams offered the hydroelectric power needed, while the flat but rocky terrain would provide stable foundations for the huge plutonium production buildings. The site comprised nearly 780 square miles and was far enough inland to meet security requirements. The existing transportation facilities could quickly be improved and labour in the Pacific Northwest was readily available. Groves accepted the committee's unanimous recommendation and gave the go-ahead for the Hanford Engineer Works, codenamed Site W.

Now that DuPont would be building the plutonium production complex in the Northwest, Compton saw no reason for any pile facilities in Oak Ridge and proposed to conduct all Met Lab research in either Chicago or Argonne. DuPont, on the other hand, continued to support a pilot plant at Oak Ridge and asked the Met Lab scientists to operate it. Compton complained that he did not have sufficient technical staff to do this. He was also reluctant because his scientists were grumbling that their laboratory was becoming little more than a subsidiary of DuPont. But in the end, Compton knew Met Lab would have to go along with DuPont, which simply did not have sufficient expertise to operate the pilot plant on its own.

Changing priorities

In the autumn of 1942, planning sessions at Met Lab led to the decision to build a second Fermi pile at Argonne as soon as his experiments on the first were completed. They would also proceed with the design of the Mae West helium-cooled unit. When DuPont engineers assessed the Met Lab's plans afterwards, they agreed that helium should be given first priority. Heavy water came second and they called for an all-out effort to produce more of this highly effective moderator. Bismuth and water were ranked third and fourth in DuPont's analysis.

Priorities changed when Fermi's calculations demonstrated a higher value for k than anyone had anticipated. Met Lab scientists concluded that a water-cooled pile was now feasible, while DuPont shifted its interest to air-cooling. Since a helium-cooled unit shared important design characteristics with an air-cooled one, Greenewalt pointed out that building an air-cooled pilot plant at Oak Ridge would contribute significantly to designing the full-scale facilities at Hanford.

DuPont outlined the general specifications for the air-cooled pilot plant and chemical separation facilities in early 1943. The pile would comprise a massive graphite block, protected by several feet of concrete. It would have hundreds of horizontal channels cut in it and filled with uranium slugs that would be surrounded by air to cool them. New slugs pushed into the channels on the face of the pile would force the irradiated ones at the rear to fall out into a bucket that was underwater. The buckets of irradiated slugs would be left to undergo radio-active decay for several weeks, then they would be moved along an underground canal into the chemical separation facility where the plutonium would be extracted with remote-controlled equipment.

The water-cooled pile

Meanwhile, Met Lab began designing a water-cooled pile for the full-scale plutonium plant. Initially, they continued with the Wigner-Young design with vertical pipes. Then, taking their cue from the DuPont engineers, they switched to a horizontal configuration with uranium slugs sealed in aluminium cans inside aluminium tubes. The water would also run through the tubes, cooling the pile. Containing 200 tons of uranium and 1200 tons of graphite, the pile would need 75,000 gallons of water a minute to cool it.

Greenewalt's initial response to the water-cooled design was guarded. He worried that pressure might build up and lead to water boiling in the tubes. There was also a problem with corrosion. But there were more worries about the proposed helium-cooled model. Greenewalt feared that the shell could not be made vacuum-tight, that the pile would be extremely difficult to operate and that the compressors would not be ready in time for use at Hanford. DuPont engineers conceded that Greenewalt's fears were well grounded. Late in February, Greenewalt reluctantly concluded that the Met Lab's water-cooled model, though it had its problems, was superior to DuPont's helium-cooled arrangement and decided to go with the water-cooled design.

Met Lab had won the pile design competition, but it was fast becoming overshadowed by developments at Oak Ridge and Hanford. Fermi continued to work on CP-1, the original Stagg Field pile, hoping to determine the exact value of k. Subsequent experiments were carried out at the Argonne site using CP-2, which had been built with material from CP-1. These focused on neutron-capture probabilities, control systems and instrument reliability. But once the production facilities at Oak Ridge and Hanford were underway, Met Lab research took a back seat and the scientists there found themselves serving primarily as consultants for DuPont.

Chemical extraction

While the Met Lab physicists chafed under the DuPont yoke, a better relationship existed between the chemists and DuPont.

Seaborg and Cooper continued to work well together. Enough progress was made in the pilot plant for the lanthanum-fluoride process in late 1942 that DuPont moved into the plant design stage and converted the pilot plant for the bismuth phosphate method.

By late May 1943, DuPont were pressing for a decision on the plutonium extraction method that was going to be used in production. Greenewalt chose the bismuth-phosphate method, though Seaborg could find little to distinguish between the two. Greenewalt decided against using lanthanum fluoride because of its corrosiveness and Seaborg guaranteed that he could extract at least 50 per cent of the plutonium using bismuth phosphate. DuPont then began constructing the chemical separation pilot plant at Oak Ridge, while Seaborg continued refining the bismuth-phosphate method.

It was now Cooper's job to design the pile as well as the plutonium extraction facilities at Oak Ridge. These were both complicated engineering tasks made even more difficult by high levels of radiation produced by the process. Not only did Cooper have to oversee the design and fabrication of parts for yet another new Manhattan Project technology, he had to do so with an eye toward planning the Hanford facility. Safety was a major consideration because of the hazards of working with plutonium, which was highly radioactive. Uranium, a much less active element than plutonium, posed far fewer safety problems.

In July 1942, Compton set up a health division at Met Lab under Robert S. Stone, who had pioneered the use of fast neutrons for malignant disease. Stone established emission standards and conducted experiments on radiation hazards, providing valuable planning information for the Oak Ridge and Hanford facilities.

Construction at Oak Ridge

DuPont broke ground for the X-10 complex at Oak Ridge in February 1943. The site would include an air-cooled experimental pile, a pilot chemical separation plant and support facilities. Cooper produced blueprints for the chemical separation plants in time for construction to begin in March. A series of huge concrete cells, the first of which sat under the pile, extended to one storey above ground. Aluminium cans containing uranium slugs would drop out of the pile into the first cell of the chemical separation facility where they would be dissolved chemically, then go through the extraction process.

The pile building went up during the spring and summer. It was a huge concrete shell 7 feet thick with hundreds of holes for uranium slugs to be put in. The Aluminum Company of American (Alcoa) was working on enclosing the U-235 in aluminium sheaths, but many cans failed their vacuum tests because of faulty welds.

In late October, DuPont completed construction and tests of the X-10 pile at Oak Ridge. After thousands of slugs were loaded, the pile went critical in the early morning of 4 November. By the end of the month, it was producing plutonium even though only half of the channels filled with uranium.

During the next several months, Compton gradually raised the power level of the pile, increasing its plutonium yield. Chemical separation techniques using the bismuth phosphate process were so successful that Los Alamos began receiving plutonium samples in the spring. The fission studies of these samples at Los Alamos during summer 1944 heavily influenced the design of bomb.

Hanford takes shape

Colonel Matthias had returned to Hanford to set up a temporary office on 22 February 1943. His orders were to purchase 500,000 acres in and around the Hanford-Pasco-White Bluffs area. It was a sparsely populated region where shepherding and farming were the main activities. Many of the area's landowners rejected initial offers for their land and tried to take the army to court, but Matthias usually settled out of court as time meant more than money to the Manhattan Project.

Once the land had been bought, the three water-cooled piles, designated B, D and F, would be built about 6 miles apart along the south bank of the Columbia River. The four chemical separation plants, built in pairs, would be constructed nearly 10 miles south of the piles, while a facility to produce slugs and perform tests would be built around 20 miles southeast of the separation plants, near the town of Richland. Temporary quarters for construction workers would be put up in Hanford, which was converted into a construction camp, while permanent facilities for other personnel would be located down the road in Richland, a safe distance from the production and separation plants.

During summer 1943, Hanford became the Manhattan Project's newest atomic boomtown. Thousands of workers poured in. But while well situated from a logistical point of view, Hanford was a sea of tents and wooden barracks where there was little to do and nowhere to go.

DuPont and the army co-ordinated efforts to recruit labourers from all over the country, but even with a relative labour surplus in the Pacific Northwest, shortages of manpower plagued the project. Conditions improved during the second half of the year, with the addition of recreational facilities. Workers' pay increased and services improved for Hanford's population, which reached 50,000 by the summer of

1944. Hanford still resembled a frontier mining town, but the rate of worker turnover dropped substantially.

Ground-breaking for the water-cooling plant for the 100-B pile, the westernmost of the three, took place on 27 August, less than two weeks before Italy's surrender to the Allies on 8 September. On 10 October, work gangs began laying the first of 390 tons of structural steel, 17,400 cubic yards of concrete, 50,000 concrete blocks and 71,000 concrete bricks. That was just to make the 40 foot windowless building the pile sat in.

Work on the pile itself began in February 1944, with the base and shield being completed by mid-May. It took another month to put the graphite pile in place and install the top shield, and two more months to wire and pipe the pile and connect it to the various monitoring and control devices.

Problems at Hanford

At Los Alamos, work was being done on the firing mechanism. Essentially, to detonate an atomic bomb, all you need to do is put together a critical mass which will then explode spontaneously. Putting it together must be done rapidly, otherwise predetonation would only produce a small explosion, which would blow the bomb apart before the optimal mass was achieved. One way to do this was to use a gun to fire a fissionable projectile into a fissionable target.

This would work with U-235, but in July 1944 it was found not to be suitable for use with plutonium. By then, Pile 100-B was almost completed, along with the first chemical separation plant. Pile D was half finished, while Pile F was not yet under construction. Instead, Los Alamos were considering making implosion devices, where a hollow sphere of plutonium would be compressed to form a critical mass. However, no one yet

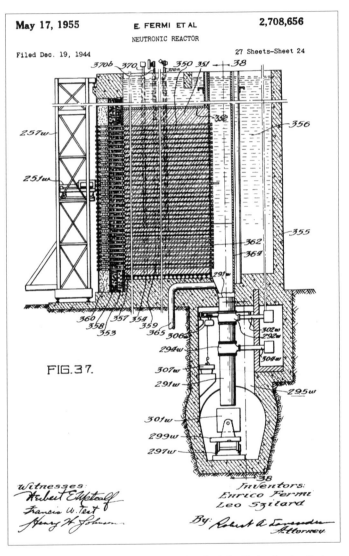

Enrico Fermi and Leo Szilard filed a US patent for their atomic pile in 1944. They had to wait until 1955 until it was approved.

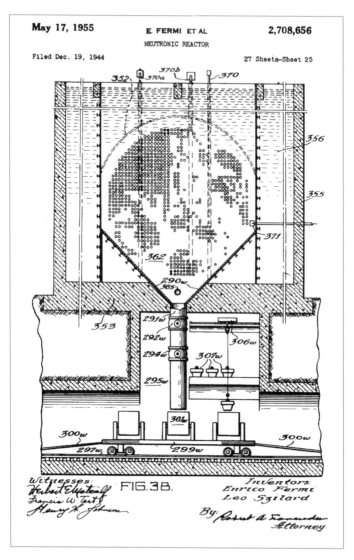

May 17, 1955   E. FERMI ET AL   2,708,656
NEUTRONIC REACTOR

Filed Dec. 19, 1944   27 Sheets—Sheet 25

FIG.3B.

Witnesses:

Inventors:
Enrico Fermi
Leo Szilard

By: Attorney

In their application, Fermi and Szilard said they had discovered the principles required for the successful construction of neutronic reactors.

knew exactly how much plutonium would be needed. Would the three piles produce enough to make a weapon?

Fermi placed the first slug in Pile 100-B on 13 September 1944. Final checks on the pile seemed satisfactory, and the scientists could only cross their fingers. Once the pile was operational, the intense radioactivity would make any further adjustments impossible.

Loading the first batch of slugs and taking measurements took two weeks. From just after midnight until around 3am on 27 September, the pile ran at a power level considerably higher than any previous chain reaction, though still only at a fraction of design capacity. But after three hours the power level began to fall. It continued until the pile stopped completely on the evening of 28 September. The next morning the reaction began again, reached the previous day's level, but then dropped off once more.

Xenon poisoning

Hanford scientists were at a loss to explain why the pile failed to maintain a chain reaction, but the DuPont engineers worked out that it was caused by 'xenon poisoning'. One of the pile's fission products was an isotope of xenon with an atomic mass of 135. It captured neutrons faster than the pile could produce them, so as the level of xenon built up it caused a gradual shutdown of the pile. Then, when the chain reaction shutdown was complete, the xenon decayed. The neutrons began to flow freely and the pile started up again.

Luckily, regardless of the objections of some of the scientists, DuPont had installed a large number of extra tubes. When these were loaded with slugs, Pile 100-B would reach a power level high enough to overwhelm the xenon poisoning. Success was achieved when the first irradiated slugs were discharged from Pile 100-B on Christmas Day, 1944.

Transportation

At Hanford, the irradiated uranium slugs would drop into water pools 16½ feet deep behind the piles, until the most intense radioactivity died away as short-lived fission products decayed. The pools glowed blue with what is known as Cherenkov radiation. Then the slugs would be moved in shielded casks on remotely controlled railroad cars to a storage facility 5 miles away. From there, they would be trans-ported to their final destination – one of the two chemical separation plants, 200-West and 200-East. The two plants that made up 200-West were designated T and U. The 200-East complex had just a single plant, unit B, as the planned fourth chemical separation plant was not built.

The Hanford chemical separation facilities were massively scaled-up versions of those at Oak Ridge, each containing sepa-ration and concentration buildings in addition to waste storage areas and ventilation facilities to remove radioactive and poisonous gases. Labour shortages and the lack of completed blueprints forced DuPont to stop work on the 200 areas in summer 1943 and concentrate its efforts on Pile 100-B, so progress on the construction of chemical separation plants in 1943 was limited to digging two huge holes in the ground.

The Queen Marys

The 221T and 221U chemical separation buildings in the 200-West complex were finished by December 1944. In spring 1945, 221B, their counterpart in 200-East, was completed. They were nicknamed Queen Marys by the workers who built them. These separation buildings were awe-inspiring canyon-like structures 800 feet long, 65 feet wide and 80 feet high. By comparison, the ocean liner *Queen Mary*, launched in 1934, was 1019 feet long, 118 feet wide and 181 feet high. She is now moored as a tourist attraction at Long Beach, California.

The Queen Marys at Hanford were large concrete boxes with concrete walls 7 feet thick. Each one contained 40 cells, with 6-foot thick lids weighing 35 tons that could be removed by an overhead crane that ran the length of the building. When they arrived at the Queen Marys, the irradiated slugs would be dissolved in hot nitric acid. The resulting solution would be syphoned into a catch tank using steam jets – a low-maintenance substitute for pumps.

There were three phases to the chemical separation: solution, precipitation and centrifugal removal of the precipitation. These were performed in tanks, precipitators and centrifuges made of corrosion-resistant stainless steel. The process would be repeated as the radioactive material moved down the building.

Operators sat behind thick concrete shielding and manipulated remote control equipment by looking through television monitors and periscopes from an upper gallery. Even with massive concrete lids on the process pools, added precautions against exposure to radiation were needed and influenced all aspects of plant design.

Once the Queen Marys were contaminated with radioactivity, no repair crews could enter them. All maintenance had to be done by remote control. The operators were trained at DuPont in Delaware, at Oak Ridge and on mock-ups at Hanford. One hundred of them who arrived at Hanford in October 1944 were then asked to install the processing equipment in the first completed separation building by remote control, as if it were already radioactive. This improved their remote-manipulation skills.

'When the Queen Marys began to function, dissolving the irradiated slugs in concentrated nitric acid,' said physicist Leona Marshall, the only woman present at the first nuclear chain reaction in Chicago, 'great plumes of brown fumes blossomed above the concrete canyons, climbed thousands of feet into the air, and drifted sideways as they cooled, blown by winds aloft.'

Construction of the chemical concentration buildings at Hanford – 224-T, 224-U and 224-B – was less of a problem as relatively little radioactivity was involved. Work was not started on them until late in 1944. The 200-West units were finished in early October, the 200-East unit in February 1945.

Modifications

In the Queen Marys, bismuth phosphate was used to carry the plutonium through the long succession of process pools. The concentration stage was then designed to separate it off. However, reports from the Oak Ridge pilot plant showed that bismuth phosphate was not suitable for use in the concentration process, though Seaborg's original choice, lanthanum fluoride, worked quite well. Accordingly, modifications were made to the concentration facilities at Hanford.

The final step in plutonium extraction was isolation of the substance itself. It was performed in a more typical laboratory setting with little radiation present and it was found that another method of separation developed at Met Lab that used peroxide worked better, producing a small quantity of highly purified plutonium nitrate. The radioactive waste was stored on site in underground tanks, while the nitrate would be prepared to be shipped to Los Alamos and converted to metal.

When the 221-T separation began operation on 26 December 1944, the yields were 60–75 per cent. By February 1945, they had reached 90 per cent.

By the end of January 1945, the first batch of plutonium nitrate underwent further concentration in the completed chemical isolation building, where remaining impurities were successfully removed.

Matthias then carried the first small batch of plutonium nitrate by train from Portland to Los Angeles, where he turned it over to a security courier from Los Alamos. It arrived there on 2 February. After that, small subcritical batches in metal containers within wooden crates were despatched by Army ambulance, in convoy, via Boise, Salt Lake City, Grand Junction and Pueblo to Los Alamos, New Mexico.

Chapter Seven
Los Alamos

Once Oak Ridge and Hanford were up and running, it was the job of Robert Oppenheimer at Los Alamos to use the material they provided to make an atomic bomb. The operation there was code-named Project Y.

Oppenheimer had spent the first three months of 1943 tirelessly crisscrossing the country in an attempt to put together a first-rate staff, an effort that proved highly successful. Even Bacher signed on, though he promised to resign the moment militarization occurred. Rabi did not move to Los Alamos, though he became a valuable consultant.

As soon as Oppenheimer moved into Los Alamos in mid-March, recruits began arriving from universities across the US, including the universities in California, Minnesota, Chicago, Princeton, Stanford, Purdue, Columbia and Iowa State, while still others came from the Met Lab, the Massachusetts Institute of Technology and the National Bureau of Standards. Virtually overnight Los Alamos became another frontier boomtown – though more of an ivory tower variety – as scientists and their families moved in. Along with them came all the equipment of nuclear physics, including two Van de Graaff generators, a Cockcroft-Walton accelerator and a cyclotron. These were brought in pieces by rail to Santa Fe, then carted up the single primitive road that led to Los Alamos, where this most remote outpost of the Manhattan Project became known as 'the Hill'.

Life on the Hill

Initially, the environment at Los Alamos was spartan. The scientists and their families lived in temporary housing and ate boxed lunches – quite a contrast to the comfortable campuses they were used to. Nevertheless, work quickly got underway, even while the Corps of Engineers struggled to provide the civilized amenities.

Though the properties of uranium were reasonably well understood, those of plutonium were less so, and the idea that fission could produce an explosion was still entirely theoretical. It was generally accepted that U-235 produced, statistically, 2.2 secondary neutrons when it fissioned, but while Seaborg's team had demonstrated in March 1941 that plutonium underwent induced fission when bombarded with neutrons, it was not yet known if plutonium released secondary neutrons at all. And if it did, would there be enough of them to produce a chain reaction?

The theoretical consensus was that chain reactions took place with sufficient speed to produce a powerful release of energy and not just blow up the critical mass itself, but only experiments could test the theory. The optimum size and shape of the critical mass had yet to be determined. After that the optimum effective mass still had to be established. It was not enough just to start a chain reaction in a critical mass; it was necessary to start one in a mass that would release the greatest possible amount of energy before the bomb itself was destroyed in the explosion.

The gadget

Along with calculations on uranium and plutonium fission, chain reactions and critical and effective masses, work needed to be done on the ordnance aspects of the bomb, or 'the gadget' as it came to be known. Two subcritical masses of fissionable material would have to come together to form a supercritical mass for an explosion to occur. Furthermore, they had to come together in a precise manner and at high speed.

The construction of the bomb had to ensure that the highly unstable subcritical masses did not predetonate because of spontaneously emitted neutrons or neutrons produced by alpha particles reacting with lightweight impurities. There was a danger that even a cosmic ray could set it off.

The chances of predetonation could be reduced by purification of the fissionable material. There would have to be a high-speed firing system capable of achieving velocities of 3000 feet per second, otherwise the chain reaction would begin, blowing the bomb apart before the maximum effect could be achieved. With U-235 it was possible to build a simple gun that would fire one subcritical mass into the other, but this method would work for plutonium only if absolute purification of plutonium could be achieved.

Unable to purify the plutonium sufficiently, bomb designers came up with the idea of using high explosives to compress a sphere of plutonium into a supercritical mass, releasing neutrons and causing a chain reaction.

The hydrogen bomb

It was also known, theoretically, that it would be possible to create a fusion, or hydrogen, bomb. Just as when heavy nuclei break up, or fission, energy is given off, so when light

The German-born, British, theoretical physicist Klaus Fuchs (1911–88) who was convicted of supplying information about the Manhattan Project to the Soviet Union.

nuclei are forced together by immense temperatures and pressures, they fuse, giving off energy. The fusion of hydrogen atoms, producing helium, is the energy that powers the sun. If it could be made, a thermonuclear, or fusion, device would be considerably more powerful than either a uranium or plutonium device, though it would need a fission bomb as a detonator.

Research on the hydrogen bomb – or the Super, as it was called at Los Alamos – was always a distant second in priority, but Oppenheimer thought that it was too important to ignore. After considerable deliberation, he gave Edward Teller permission to devote himself to the Super.

To make up for the absence of Teller, Rudolf Peierls, one of a group of British scientists who joined the Los Alamos staff at the beginning of 1944, was added to Bethe's theory group in mid-1944. Another member of the British contingent was the Soviet agent Klaus Fuchs, who had been passing nuclear information to the Russians since 1942 and continued doing so until 1949 when he was caught and convicted of espionage.

Another Lewis Committee

The first few months at Los Alamos were occupied with briefings on nuclear physics for the technical staff, along with the planning research priorities and organizing the laboratory. Groves called once again on Warren Lewis to head a committee, this time to evaluate the Los Alamos programme.

The committee's recommendations resulted in the co-ordinated effort envisioned by those who advocated a unified laboratory for bomb research. Fermi took control of critical mass experiments and worked on the standardization of measurement techniques. Work on the purification of plutonium, begun at the Met Lab, became high priority at Los Alamos, where increased attention was paid to metallurgy. The committee also recommended that an engineering division be established to collaborate with physicists on bomb design and fabrication.

As a result, the laboratory was organized into four divisions: theoretical physics under Hans A. Bethe; experimental physics under Robert F. Bacher; chemistry and metallurgy under Joseph W. Kennedy; and ordnance under navy captain William S. 'Deke' Parsons. Like other Manhattan Project installations, Los Alamos soon began to expand beyond all expectations.

As director, Oppenheimer had to deal with problems both large and small. As well as building a bomb, he had to attend to numerous mundane matters such as the allocation of living quarters, mail censorship, salaries, promotions, and generally making life bearable in a intellectual pressure cooker with few social amenities. Oppenheimer relied on a group of advisers to help him keep the big picture in focus, while a committee made up of Los Alamos group leaders provided day-to-day communications between divisions.

Early progress

Early experiments on both uranium and plutonium provided encouraging results. It was found that uranium emitted neutrons in less than a billionth of a second. This was just enough time, in the world of nuclear physics, to create an efficient explosion.

In December 1943, Emilio Segrè showed that if the bomb was shielded from cosmic rays, the uranium would not have to be so highly purified and the subcritical masses would not have to be brought together as quickly as previously thought. That meant muzzle velocity for the scaled-down artillery piece that was going to be used could be lower, so the gun could be shorter and lighter.

Segrè's tests on the first samples of plutonium demonstrated that it emitted even more neutrons than uranium due to the spontaneous fission of plutonium-240. Both theory and experimental data now agreed that a bomb using either element would detonate if it could be designed and fabricated to the correct size and shape. Many details remained to be worked out, but first they had to calculate how much U-235 or plutonium would be needed for an explosive device.

Bacher's engineering division used particle accelerators to work out the probabilities of a nuclear reaction taking place. These measurements were needed to calculate critical and efficient masses. They also compiled data that helped identify materials to use as a 'tamper'. In mining, for example, mud is tamped into drill holes to plug them and confine conventional explosives. In a nuclear bomb, a tamper is required to reflect neutrons back into the core and enhance the efficiency of the explosion. A lot of this work was methodical, painstaking and tedious.

The chemists' job was to purify the U-235 and plutonium, reduce them to metals, and process the tamper material. It was thought that only highly purified uranium and plutonium would be safe from predetonation. However, after Segrè's discovery, the purification standards for uranium were relatively modest, so the chemical division was able to focus its effort on the lesser known plutonium, and it had made substantial progress with a multi-step precipitation process by the summer of 1944.

The metallurgy division had to turn the purified compounds of U-235 and plutonium into metal. Here, too, significant progress was made by summer as the metallurgists adapted a technique initially developed at Iowa State University.

In ordnance engineering, Parsons and his staff set out to design two artillery pieces of relatively standard specifications – one for a uranium weapon and one for a plutonium bomb. The projectiles needed to achieve high velocities, but the guns could have light barrels; they did not have to be durable as they would be fired only once. Again early efforts centred on the plutonium weapon, which required a higher muzzle velocity due to its higher risk of predetonation. Two plutonium guns arrived in March and were field-tested successfully. That same month, two uranium guns were ordered.

Early implosion work

Happy with the gun method of detonation, Parsons assigned studies of implosion a low priority. Nevertheless, experimental physicist Seth H. Neddermeyer was determined to undertake implosion tests. The problem he found was to achieve symmetrical implosions. The high-explosive shell would melt the metal core, so it was difficult to compress the material uniformly without some of it squirting out of the side. Parsons mocked: 'To my mind he is gradually working up to what I shall refer to as the Beer-Can Experiment. As soon as he gets his explosives properly organized, we will see this done. The point to watch for is whether he can blow in a beer can without splattering the beer.'

The Princeton mathematician John von Neumann, another Hungarian refugee, visited Los Alamos late in 1943. He had been working on the complex hydrodynamics of shock waves from shaped charges which were being used in the bazooka, the American infantry weapon. The focused explosion of this shoulder-fired weapon could take out a tank.

'Johnny was quite interested in high explosives,' said Teller who had known von Neumann as a youth. 'In my discussions with him, some crude calculations were made. The calculation is indeed simple as long as you assume that the material to be accelerated is incompressible, which is the usual assumption about solid matter . . . In materials driven by high explosives, pressures of more than 100,000 atmospheres occur . . . This is more than the pressure at the centre of the earth and it was known to me (but not to Johnny), that at these pressures, iron is not incompressible. In fact I had rough figures for the relevant compressibilities. The result of all this was that in the implosion significant compressions will occur, a point which had not been previously discussed.'

It was already clear that by squeezing a hollow shell of plutonium into a solid ball, you could put together a critical mass much quicker than you could firing it from a gun. But von Neumann and Teller realized that by using more violent explosions than Neddermeyer had yet attempted, it would be possible to squeeze a solid subcritical sphere of plutonium to such unearthly densities that it would detonate. This would avoid the problems of compressing hollow shells. The high speed of the compression would prevent predetonation; the plutonium would not have to be so pure and you would need less of it. In other words, you could make a more reliable bomb more quickly. It would also be smaller, and therefore much easier to fit in a plane.

Von Neumann and Teller's theories excited Oppenheimer, who assigned Parsons's deputy, George B. Kistiakowsky, the task of perfecting implosion techniques. A Harvard chemistry professor, Kistiakowsky was from Kiev in the Ukraine and had fled to Germany during the Russian Civil War of 1918–20. After getting his doctorate at Berlin University, he emigrated to the United States. In 1940, he had been studying explosions for the National Defense Research Committee.

'By 1943, I thought I knew something about them,' he said. 'They could be made into precision instruments, a view which was very different from that of military ordnance.'

A navy man, Parsons tried to run his division as a military unit. This suited neither Neddermeyer nor Kistiakowsky, who were largely allowed to get on with things on their own. Meanwhile, Parsons directed his own efforts towards developing the hardware of the bomb – the arming and wiring mechanisms and fusing devices. Working with the US Army

Air Force, Parsons's group developed two bomb models by
March 1944 and began testing them with B-29 bombers. Thin
Man, named for President Roosevelt, was the design carrying
the plutonium gun, while Fat Man, named for Winston
Churchill, was an implosion prototype. Segrè's lighter,
smaller uranium bomb was later dubbed Little Boy,
Thin Man's brother.

Elimination of Thin Man

Thin Man was eliminated four months later because of the
detonation problem. Seaborg had warned that when
plutonium-239 was irradiated for a length of time it was
likely to pick up an additional neutron, transforming it into
plutonium-240. The spontaneous fission of plutonium-240
increased the danger of predetonation. It was calculated that
the bullet and target in the plutonium weapon would melt
before they came together. Measurements taken at Oak Ridge
confirmed the presence of plutonium-240 in the plutonium
produced in the experimental pile, so on 17 July work on the
plutonium gun method was cancelled. Plutonium could be used
only in an implosion device, but in the summer of 1944 an
implosion weapon still looked like a long shot.

Abandoning the plutonium gun had eliminated one shortcut
to making the bomb. This meant that the estimates of when a
bomb could be delivered that Bush had given the President in
1943 would have to be revised. The new timetable was
presented to Roosevelt's Army Chief of Staff, General Marshall,
by Groves on 7 August 1944, two months after the Allied landings on Normandy on 6 June. It said that small implosion
weapons using uranium or plutonium would be ready in the
second quarter of 1945, if experiments proved satisfactory.
Groves was more confident that a uranium gun bomb could be

delivered by 1 August 1945, and another one or two more by the end of that year. Marshall and Groves acknowledged that German surrender might take place by summer 1945, making it likely that Japan would be the atomic bomb's first target.

Chapter Eight
Deadline

Expenditures on the Manhattan Project had reached $100 million a month by mid-1944. No one was sure that Groves' deadline of 1 August 1945 could really be reached. Indeed, with the Germans now in retreat on all fronts and the Japanese being pushed back in the Pacific, it was not certain that a weapon would be ready for use in the war at all.

Operational problems plagued the Y-12 electromagnetic facility that was just coming on line. The K-25 gaseous diffusion plant threatened to become an expensive white elephant as a suitable barrier had not yet been manufactured. And while the Hanford piles and separation facilities looked promising, there was a shortage of uranium slugs to feed into the pile. Even assuming that enough uranium or plutonium could be delivered by the production facilities, there was no guarantee that the Los Alamos laboratory would be able to design and build weapons in time.

Progress at Oak Ridge

During the winter of 1944–45, progress was made at Oak Ridge. The production facilities improved their performance and

Nichols co-ordinated the complicated feed schedule to maximize output of enriched uranium, using the electromagnetic, thermal diffusion and gaseous diffusion processes in tandem.

Nine Alpha and three Beta racetracks were up and running. While they were not working up to design potential, they were becoming significantly more reliable thanks to maintenance improvements and various chemical refinements introduced by Tennessee Eastman.

The S-50 thermal diffusion plant being built by the H. K. Ferguson Company of Cleveland, Ohio. Graves had given the company just 90 days to complete the project – just half the time the company had optimistically estimated would be necessary. With the help of creative shortcuts, such as using passenger trains to deliver some construction materials, Ferguson met its seemingly impossible deadline. By September 1944, the S-50 enrichment plant was almost finished and was producing small amounts of enriched material in the racks already completed. Then a functional barrier for the K-25 gaseous diffusion plant was found and it was undergoing formal leak tests. By March 1945, Union Carbide had worked out most of the kinks in K-25 and had started recycling uranium hexafluoride through the system. S-50 was complete at the same time.

By then, the Y-12 racetracks were becoming increasingly efficient. The Beta calutrons at the electromagnetic plant were producing weapon-grade U-235 using feed from the modified Alpha racetracks and the small output from the gaseous diffusion and thermal diffusion facilities. Oak Ridge was now sending enough enriched U-235 to Los Alamos to meet experimental needs. To increase production, Groves proposed an additional gaseous diffusion plant, K-27, for low-level enrichment, and a fourth Beta track for high-level enrichment. Both were to be completed by February 1946. The war in Europe had ended at the beginning of May 1945, but it was thought that the war against Japan would not end before the summer of 1946.

Reorganization

Oppenheimer acted quickly to maximize the laboratory's efforts to master implosion. Only if the implosion method worked would the plutonium produced at Hanford be of any use. Without either a plutonium gun or implosion bomb, they would be totally dependent on a uranium bomb with its less efficient gun method, which was still to be tested.

So Oppenheimer made a major reorganization of the Los Alamos laboratory in July 1944 to concentrate work on the final development of an implosion device. Robert Bacher took over G – for gadget – Division to experiment with implosion and design a bomb. George Kistiakowsky would lead X Division, working on the explosive components. Hans Bethe continued to head up theoretical studies, while Deke Parsons now focused on overall bomb construction and delivery.

Field tests performed with U-235 prototypes in late 1944 showed that the gun method would work in the uranium bomb and it seemed certain that enough U-235 would come from Oak Ridge to make a gun-type nuclear device by the 1 August deadline. The plutonium produced at such expense and effort at Hanford would not fit into wartime planning unless there was a breakthrough in implosion technology.

At the same time, Los Alamos shifted from research to development and production. No one had yet worked out a detailed engineering plan of how to manufacture a finished bomb.

The USAAF gets ready

At the US Army Air Force, training could wait no longer and in September at Wendover Field in western Utah, 29-year-old Lieutenant Colonel Paul W. Tibbets began drilling the 393rd Bombardment Squadron of the 509th Composite Wing in test drops with 5500-pound orange dummy bombs, nicknamed pumpkins, on the Great Salt Lake. These had the same ballistic characteristics as Fat Man.

Tibbets was recognized as the best bomber pilot in the Air Force. He had led the first B-17 bombing mission from England over occupied Europe. Then he had flown General Dwight D. Eisenhower to his command post in Gibraltar before the Allied landings in northwest Africa and conducted the first bombing raids there afterwards. More recently, he had been a test pilot for Boeing's new B-29 Superfortress and worked with the physics department of the University of New Mexico to determine how well the B-29 could defend itself against fighter attack.

In September 1944, Parsons and Norman Ramsey, a Columbia physicist in charge of the delivery group, briefed Tibbets. He was then told by his commanding officer, Major General Uzal Girard Ent, 'You have to put together an outfit and deliver this weapon. We don't know anything about it yet. We don't know what it can do . . . You've got to mate it to the airplane and determine the tactics, the training and the ballistics – everything. These are all parts of your problem. This thing is going to be very big. I believe it has the potential and possibility of ending the war.'

Tibbets's delivery programme was to be code-named 'Silverplate'. If Tibbets needed anything, he was to use that magic word, which had been accorded the highest priority in the service.

In June 1945, Tibbets and his command moved to Tinian Island in the Marianas, where the Navy SeaBees had built the world's largest airport to accommodate the new Superfortresses, which had been manufactured specially to bomb Japan. From there, Tibbets and his crew began flying bombing missions over Japan to familiarize themselves with the target area. By then, the home islands had been bombed for more than six months.

Bombs fall on Tokyo

It was with the fall of Saipan in the Marianas in July 1944 that
the Japanese mainland had at last come within the range of the
Superfortress. The first flight of 100 B-29s took off from the
base there on 12 November 1944 and bombed Tokyo, the first
air raid on the city since 1942, when 16 B-25s under the
command of General James H. Doolittle took off from the
aircraft carrier USS *Hornet*, flew the 600 miles to Japan,
dropped their bombs and, without enough fuel to return, flew
on eastwards to land behind friendly lines in China.

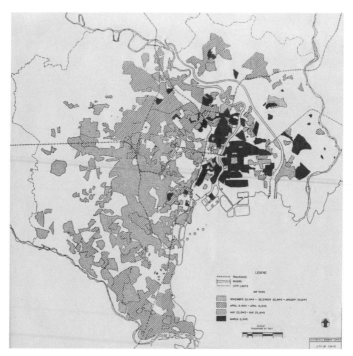

*Map of the US strategic bombing campaign on Tokyo from 29
November 1944 to 25 May 1945.*

French journalist Robert Guillain was in Toyko and witnessed the raid in November 1944.

'Suddenly there was an odd, rhythmic buzzing that filled the night with a deep, powerful pulsation and made my whole house vibrate: the marvellous sound of the B-29s passing invisibly through a nearby corner of the sky, pursued by the barking of anti-aircraft fire,' he wrote. 'I went up on my terrace roof . . . The B-29s caught in the sweeping searchlight beams went tranquilly on their way followed by the red flashes of ack-ack bursts which could not reach them at that altitude. A pink light spread across the horizon, behind a near hill, growing bigger, bloodying the whole sky. Other red splotches lit up like nebulas elsewhere in the horizon. It was soon to be a familiar sight. Feudal Tokyo was called Edo, and the people there had always been terrified by the frequent accidental fires they euphemistically called 'flowers of Edo'. That night, all Tokyo began to blossom.'

The bombing came as no surprise to the Japanese people. Correspondents in Germany had described the havoc wrought by Allied bombers on German cities, which were known to be much more solidly built than Japanese towns. An officer captured in the Philippines said, 'The people's reaction is: "What can we do when the authorities do nothing? Our cities will be simply wiped out." Similarly the government's attempt to harden people's nerves and prepare them against panic are having only negative results. I myself know families who would not allow their children to go far from home on sunny days last summer when everybody constantly expected air raids. The danger of air raids is freely and constantly discussed in the secrecy of family circles and fear is undisguised among friends in universities, factories and practically all circles where one can talk frankly.'

Tokyo's shallow subways could not afford much protection against heavy bombs. Other cities lacked underground shelters and those that were built, in spite of a severe shortage of construction materials, were largely inadequate. The emphasis was laid on fire-fighting and all civilians were to train for two hours every morning from 5am. But the methods used were primitive; the authorities gave prizes to those who were able to throw a bucket of water the highest.

The Japanese minister of home affairs in 1945 said, 'The reason we had no definite policy of air-raid shelter protection for the citizens is that we did not unduly wish to alarm our citizens concerning the necessity for underground shelters as we feared it would interfere with normal routine life and have some effect on war production. We did encourage citizens who could afford it to build their own family air-raid shelters.'

Even so, the Japanese government made civilians a legitimate target. As large factories were easy to hit by low-level bombing, lathes and other items of machinery were moved out to workers' homes, so that every house became a potential munitions factory.

Shortages

In the final push to make a bomb, Los Alamos found itself short of personnel, particularly physicists. Getting the necessary supplies was also a problem. The procurement system designed to protect the secrecy of the Los Alamos project led to frustrating delays on top of the normal wartime shortages. For Oppenheimer, this was a constant headache. It was difficult even to contact supply sources from the remote laboratory and few academic scientists are well versed in logistics.

Groves and Conant were determined not to let petty problems impede the bomb effort. In the autumn of 1944, Conant shipped as many scientists as could be spared from Chicago and Oak Ridge to Los Alamos and hired every civilian machinist he could find. Hartley Rowe, an experienced industrial engineer, was co-opted to help ease the transition from research to production. Los Alamos also arranged for a rocket research team at the California Institute of Technology to aid procurement, providing test fuses and contributing to component development.

Enlisted men were brought in to supplement the workforce. These GIs were known as SEDS, for Special Engineering Detachment. It was not a popular posting. The area was full of yucca plants as sharp as samurai swords, and the men had to shake centipedes and scorpions from their boots in the morning. The water was fouled with gypsum, a drastic purgative. Groves ordered only cold showers for the men at the test site, who were later to receive an award for having the lowest venereal disease rate of any unit in the entire US Army.

Freezing gun design

Weapon design for the uranium gun bomb was frozen in February 1945. By then, confidence in it was high enough that further tests prior to combat use were thought to be unnecessary. All the assets at Los Alamos were now concentrated on implosion.

The design for an implosion device was approved in March and a test of the plutonium weapon was scheduled for 4 July. Oppenheimer shifted the laboratory into high gear and assigned Allison, Bacher and Kistiakowsky to the Cow Puncher Committee, which was to 'ride herd' on the implosion weapon. He put Harvard physics professor Kenneth T. Bainbridge, recruited from MIT's radar project, in charge of Project Trinity, a new division to oversee the July test firing. Parsons headed Project Alberta, known as Project A, which had the responsibility for preparing and delivering weapons for combat.

Portrait of Kenneth Bainbridge, holding a photo of the Trinity test, 16 July 1945.

During these critical months much depended upon the ability of the chemists and metallurgists to process the uranium and plutonium into metal, which then had to be crafted to the right size and shape. Plutonium proved much harder to work with than uranium. It existed in different states, depending upon temperature, and was extremely toxic. Working under intense pressure, the chemists and metallurgists managed to develop precise techniques for processing plutonium just before it arrived in quantity from the beginning of May.

The delivery of a uranium weapon, Little Boy, by the projected date of 1 August now looked more likely than not. There would be no implosion weapon in the first half of 1945 as Groves had hoped, but things were looking good for the scheduled July test of the Fat Man plutonium bomb.

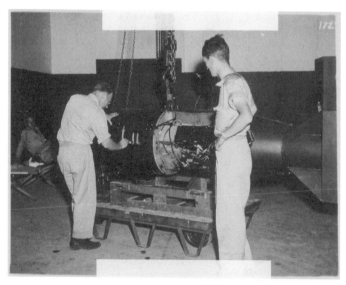

The Little Boy with Commander A. Birch (left) and Dr. Norman Foster Ramsey. Note the open case of the bomb.

Calculations provided by Bethe's theoretical group put the yield for the first weapon in the vicinity of the equivalent of 5000 tons of TNT rather than the 1000-ton estimate made in the autumn of 1944.

In the spring of 1945, with the Manhattan Project on the brink of success, the atomic bomb became an increasingly important element in America's overall strategy. A long-hoped-for weapon now seemed within reach at a time when hard decisions were being made, not only on ending the war in the Pacific, but also on the shape of the post-war world.

The German pile

As the war in Europe was coming to an end, the question remained: had the Germans got a bomb? Had they even been working on one? No one knew. In late 1943, Groves had set up a unit to find out. It was called Alsos, Greek for 'grove', and was headed by an FBI-trained army G-2 security officer, Lieutenant Colonel Boris T. Pash. He was already known to the scientists of the Manhattan Project as he had investigated the Communist activities of the staff members of Lawrence's Berkeley laboratory. He had also interrogated Oppenheimer about his Communist affiliations while recording the conversation on a hidden recording device.

In 1944 Pash set up operations in London. After the D-Day landings, he moved to Normandy. When the Americans stopped outside Paris to allow the Free French the honour of liberating the city, Pash went in with the first five French vehicles. These were tanks, while Pash's unarmoured jeep drew sniper fire. It was the first American vehicle into the city.

Pash drove directly to the Radium Institute on the Rue Pierre Curie, where he drank champagne with Frédéric Joliot. However, Joliot knew little about German research. Pash then moved on to Strasbourg, where he found a German physics laboratory installed in a building in the grounds of the city hospital. His scientific counterpart, Samuel A. Goudsmit, was a Dutch theoretical physicist from the MIT Radiation Laboratory who was also versed in criminology. He examined the documents they found there.

'It is true that no precise information was given in these documents,' Pash said, 'but there was far more than enough to get a view of the whole German uranium project. We studied the papers by candlelight for two days and nights until our eyes began to hurt . . . The conclusion was unmistakable. The evidence had proved definitely that Germany had no atom bomb and was not likely to have one in any reasonable form.'

This was not good enough for Groves. He wanted to know the whereabouts of the 1200 tons of uranium the Germans had captured in Belgium in 1940. Pash had already found 31 tons of it in a French arsenal at Toulouse, where it had been secretly diverted and stored.

Crossing the Rhine into Germany, Pash acquired a large force of men, four jeeps with machine guns mounted on them and two armoured cars, then went hunting for German atomic scientists.

'Washington wanted absolute proof that no atomic activity of which it did not know was being carried on by the Nazis,' Pash said. 'It also wanted to be sure that no prominent German scientist would evade capture or fall into the hands of the Soviet Union.'

In Heidelberg, he captured Walther Bothe, head of the Institute of Physics, along with Germany's only working cyclotron. At Stadtilm, near Weimar, he found the central office of German atomic research, though Werner Heisenberg and the rest of his group from the Kaiser Wilhelm Institute had fled south, leaving behind a small stash of uranium oxide.

Captured documents indicated that the rest of the Belgium

ore might be in a factory at Stassfurt, near Magdeburg. The British were there, but the Red Army was advancing fast and the area might fall into the Soviet zone of occupation.

Groves organized a joint British and American strike force under Lieutenant Colonel John Lansdale to move in. They went to see the Twelfth Army Group's G-2. Lansdale said, 'We outlined our proposal and advised him that if we found the material we were after we proposed to remove it and that it would be necessary that we act with the utmost secrecy and greatest dispatch inasmuch as a meeting between the Russian armies and Allied armies apparently would soon take place and the area in which the material appeared to be was a part of the proposed Russian zone of occupation. The G-2 was very perturbed at our proposal and foresaw all kinds of difficulties with the Russians and political repercussions at home. Said he must see the commanding general.'

Lansdale went to see General Omar Bradley, who was in conference with the Ninth Army Commander in whose area Stassfurt lay. Both of them gave their approval. Bradley was reported to have said 'to hell with the Russians'.

At Stassfurt, Lansdale and his team found the plant a mess, from both Allied bombing and looting by French workmen.

'After going through mountains of paper we located the *lager* or inventory of papers which disclosed the presence of the material we sought at the plant,' said Lansdale.

The ore was in barrels in an open-sided shed and had obviously been there a long time; many of the barrels were broken open. Around 1100 tons of ore was stored there in various forms, most of it the concentrates from Belgium, along with around 8 tons of uranium oxide.

Lansdale told his group to take an inventory and headed to Ninth Army headquarters, where he was assigned two trucks. He moved on to the nearest railhead in the American zone, but the commanding officer there was too busy evacuating around

10,000 Allied prisoners of war to lend him more than half-a-dozen men. Lansdale then found empty aircraft hangars nearby, where he could store the ore before it was shipped out of Germany, and had them cleared of booby traps.

Back at Stassfurt, those barrels that had not broken open were too weak to stand transportation. So Lansdale took a jeep and scouted around the country until he found a paper-bag factory which had a large stock of heavy bags. He sent back a truck and took 10,000 of them.

He also found in a mill a quantity of wire and the implements needed for closing the bags. Two days after heading out for Stassfurt, he had a large crew repacking the ore. That night they started shipping it to the railhead.

Meanwhile, Pash had discovered that Werner Heisenberg, Otto Hahn and other German scientists were in the resort town of Haigerloch in the Black Forest region of southwest Germany. This was still in enemy hands, though the French were breaking through there. Pash hastily assembled his men, who now included a battalion of combat engineers, and raced around Stuttgart in a convoy of jeeps and trucks to beat the French to Haigerloch. This was to be Alsos's first seizure of an enemy town.

When they arrived at the picturesque town straddling the Eyach River, they found white pillowcases, sheets and towels bedecking flagpoles, window shutters and broomstick handles. Plainly the people of Haigerloch wished to surrender. The team quickly located the Nazi research facility – 'an ingenious set-up that gave almost complete protection from aerial observation and bombardment'.

Pash said that as he hurried to the scene, 'I saw a box-like concrete entrance to a cave in the side of an 80-foot cliff towering above the lower level of the town. The heavy steel door was padlocked. A paper stuck on the door indicated the manager's identity . . . When the manager was brought to me, he tried to convince me that he was only an accountant. When he hesitated at my command to unlock the door, I said: "Beaston, shoot the lock off the door. If he gets in the way, shoot him." The manager opened the door.'

Inside the main chamber was a concrete pit some 10 feet in diameter. In the lid was a heavy metal shield covering the top of a thick metal cylinder. This contained a pot-shaped vessel, also made of a heavy metal. It was about 4 feet below the level of the floor. On top of the vessel was a metal frame. A German prisoner confirmed that the Americans had captured the Nazi uranium 'machine', as the German called it. It was an atomic pile.

Leaving Goudsmit and his colleagues at Haigerloch, Pash moved on to nearby Hechingen, where he picked up most of the German atomic scientists. Otto Hahn was captured in Tailfingen two days later and Werner Heisenberg was found with his family in a cottage beside a lake in Bavaria.

The pile at Haigerloch had been used for the Kaiser Wilhelm Institute's final round of neutron-multiplication studies. It had been moderated by 1½ tons of Norsk-Hydro heavy water. For fuel it used 664 cubes of metallic uranium which hung down into the water on 78 chains around a central neutron source. Early that month the KWI team had used it to produce nearly seven-fold neutron multiplication. Heisenberg calculated that a 50 per cent increase in the size of the reactor would produce a sustained chain reaction.

'The fact that the German atomic bomb was not an immediate threat', Pash wrote, 'was probably the most significant single piece of military intelligence developed throughout the war. Alone, that information was enough to justify Alsos.'

More than that, they had also prevented the Soviets from capturing the leading German atomic scientists and had acquired a significant amount of high-quality uranium ore. The batch found at Toulouse was already being processed at Oak Ridge for use in Little Boy.

From Roosevelt to Truman

On 12 April 1945, only weeks before Germany's unconditional surrender on 7 May, President Roosevelt died suddenly in Warm Springs, Georgia, and Vice President Harry S. Truman, a veteran of the United States Senate, took over the presidency.

Having been Vice President for less than three months, Truman was not privy to many of the secret war efforts Roosevelt had undertaken and had to be briefed extensively in his first weeks in office. He knew nothing of the Manhattan Project or the atomic bomb.

One of the briefings by Secretary of War Stimson, on 25 April, concerned S-1. Groves was present during part of the meeting, which traced the history of the Manhattan Project, outlined its current status and presented the timetable for testing and combat delivery. Truman asked numerous questions during the 45-minute meeting and made it clear that he understood the relevance of the atomic bomb to the military situation and forthcoming diplomatic initiatives.

By the time Truman took office, Japan was near defeat. American aircraft were attacking Japanese cities at will. The B-29 was the world's first pressurized bomber. It flew at altitudes that the few remaining Japanese fighters could not reach.

A single fire-bomb raid on Tokyo in March killed nearly 100,000 people and injured over a million. On 13 April, the Imperial Army Air Force's laboratory where early Japanese research on the atomic bomb had been done was hit. Another air attack on Tokyo in May killed 83,000. Similar attacks followed on 67 cities, including Yokohama, Kobe, Osaka, Toyama and Nagoya. As more islands fell into American hands, the bombing campaign was ramped up. According to the Japanese government's official statistics, air attacks killed 260,000 people and destroyed 2,210,000 houses, leaving 9,200,000 homeless.

President Harry S. Truman (1884-1972).

The minister in charge said, 'After the 23–24 May 1945 raid on Tokyo, civilian defence measures in that city, as well as other parts of Japan, were considered a futile effort.'

By the end of the war, Japan was surrounded by the US and British navies, shelling the ports at will. Their blockade severed the islands' supply lines. But the accepted view was that the Japanese would fight to the bitter end and an invasion of the home islands would be costly. So American policy-makers clung to the idea that the successful combat delivery of one or more atomic bombs might convince the Japanese that further resistance was futile.

There was little doubt of the determination of the Japanese

Tokyo burns a under B-29 firebomb assault, 26 May 1945.

to fight on. Tokyo radio said, 'If by any chance the enemy believed that he could demoralize the Japanese people, he has made a big mistake. The Emperor of Japan, on the morning of 18 March, deigned to pay an unexpected personal visit to the stricken districts of the Capital. He went on foot, exposing himself to the cold March wind. All the people, touched by his sympathy, renewed their determination to prosecute the war, saying: "This is a sacred war against the diabolical Americans".'

Japanese civilians were being armed with bamboo spears to defend themselves against any invasion force. This was no empty threat. American troops had suffered terribly in the face of the fanatical Japanese defence of the Pacific islands they had held. At the tiny island of Iwo Jima, the Americans came under attack by *kamikazes*, losing 6,821 killed and 19,217 wounded out of a force of 70,000. Some 20,000 Japanese were also killed.

The fighting became even more intense when the Americans

USS Bunker Hill hit by two Kamikazes in 30 seconds on 11 May 1945 off Kyushu. 372 people died and 264 were wounded.

landed on Okinawa, the first of the Japanese home islands, in April 1945. When the battle was lost, tens of thousands of civilians committed suicide rather than surrender.

The post-war position

On 6 June, Stimson again briefed Truman on S-1. The briefing summarized the consensus of the Interim Committee, set up as an advisory group on atomic research. It was charged with recommending the proper use of atomic weapons in wartime and developing a position for the United States on post-war atomic policy. The committee comprised Bush, Conant, Compton, Under Secretary of the Navy Ralph A. Bard, Assistant Secretary of State William L. Clayton and the director of the Office of War Mobilization, soon to be Secretary of State, James F. Byrnes. Oppenheimer, Fermi, Compton and Lawrence served as a scientific panel, while General Marshall represented the military.

They had met on 31 May and concluded that the United States should not share its nuclear secrets, though an accord had been made with Churchill, and should try to retain superiority in nuclear weapons in case international relations deteriorated. Most present thought that the US should protect its monopoly for the present, though they realized that the secrets could not be held for long. It was only a matter of time before other potentially hostile countries, particularly Russia, would be capable of producing atomic weapons.

There was also some discussion of free exchange of nuclear research for peaceful purposes and the international inspection system that such an exchange would require. Lawrence's suggestion that a demonstration of the atomic bomb might possibly convince the Japanese to surrender was discussed over lunch and rejected. No one knew whether the bomb would go off. If it did not, it would do much to improve Japanese morale.

If they were warned, the Japanese might put American prisoners of war in populated areas or make an all-out effort to shoot down the plane. Besides, the shock value of the new weapon would be lost. These reasons and others convinced the group that the bomb should be dropped without warning on a dual target – a munitions factory surrounded by workers' homes. Still no one realized quite how devastating the bomb would be.

On 1 June, the committee met Walter S. Carpenter of DuPont, James C. White of Tennessee Eastman, George H. Bucher of Westinghouse and James A. Rafferty of Union Carbide to get input from the contractors. This further convinced the Interim Committee that the US had a lead of three to ten years on the Soviet Union in making the bomb.

As a result, in his meeting with the president on 6 June, Stimson told Truman that the Interim Committee recommended keeping S-1 a secret until Japan had been bombed. The attack should take place as soon as possible and without warning. The president was due to meet Churchill and Joseph Stalin in the Berlin suburb of Potsdam to discuss post-war Europe on 17 July. While the British were already on board with the Manhattan Project, Truman and Stimson agreed that the president would stall if asked about atomic weapons by Stalin as it might be possible to gain concessions from Russia later in return for technical information.

Stimson told Truman that members of the Interim Committee generally held the position that international agreements should be made in which all nuclear research would be made public and a system of inspections would be devised. They were even considering domestic legislation to that effect. However, if international agreements were not forthcoming, the US should continue to produce as much fissionable material as possible to maintain its current position of superiority.

Chapter Nine
Trinity

Although the bomb had not yet been tested, a target selection group was set up in late April. It was headed by Groves and General Thomas Farrell, who had been appointed his military aide in February 1945. In late May, the committee, which comprised scientists as well as air force officers, listed Kokura Arsenal, Hiroshima, Niigata and Kyoto as the four best targets. These cities were as yet undamaged, though General Curtis LeMay's Twentieth Air Force planned to eliminate all major Japanese cities by 1 January 1946. Using a single bomb to wipe out a pristine city, it was thought, would have a profound psychological impression on the Japanese and weaken military resistance. It was also thought that by dropping the bomb on a city that had not already been damaged, it would be easier to judge just how much destruction this new weapon wrought.

Stimson vetoed Kyoto. Japan's most cherished cultural centre was full of priceless art treasures. The Allied governments had already noted the revulsion among their populations at the bombing of Dresden, so Nagasaki replaced the ancient capital in the directive issued to the Army Air Force on 25 July.

The Franck Report

While decisions about the use of the atomic bomb were being made by politicians and the military, the scientists who had made it thought they should have their say. The scientific panel of the Interim Committee was the only way that they could communicate with the policy-makers and Compton was convinced it must have a high level of participation in the decision-making process. His briefing of the Met Lab staff on the findings of the Interim Committee on 2 June led to a flurry of activity. The Met Lab's Committee on the Social and Political Implications of the Atomic Bomb, chaired by James Franck, issued a report advocating international control of atomic power as the only way to stop the arms race that would be inevitable if the United States bombed Japan without first demonstrating the weapon in an uninhabited area.

The scientific panel disagreed with the Franck Report, as the Met Lab report was known. It concluded that no technical test would convince Japan to surrender and a military demonstration of the bomb might best further the cause of peace, but held that such a demonstration should take place only after the US informed its allies – which, of course, included the Soviet Union.

On 21 June, the Interim Committee agreed with the position advanced by the scientific panel. The bomb should be used as soon as possible, without warning and against a war plant surrounded by additional buildings. As to informing allies, the Committee concluded that when Truman went to Berlin in mid July, he should mention to Stalin that the United States was preparing to use a new kind of weapon against Japan.

On 2 July 1945, President Truman listened as Stimson detailed the peace terms he had drawn up for Japan. These included demilitarization and prosecution of war criminals in exchange for governmental and economic freedom. Stimson returned to the Oval Office on 3 July and suggested that Truman broach the issue of the bomb with Stalin. It would put the Russians on notice and serve, in Stimson's words, as a 'badly needed equalizer'.

The Journey of Death

Meanwhile, the test of the plutonium weapon was rescheduled for 16 July at a barren site on the Alamogordo Bombing Range known as the Jornada del Muerto, or 'Journey of Death', 210 miles south of Los Alamos. The test and the test site were named 'Trinity' by Oppenheimer.

Groves wrote to him in 1962, asking why he had picked that name and speculating that he had chosen it because it was a name commonly given to rivers and peaks in the American West, so it would be inconspicuous. Oppenheimer replied that he had not suggested the name on those grounds.

'Why I chose the name is not clear,' he said, 'but I know what thoughts were in my mind. There is a poem of John Donne, written just before his death, which I know and love. From it a quotation:

> As West and East
> In all flatt Maps (and I am one) are one,
> So death doth touch the Resurrection.'

The poem was 'Hymn to God My God, in My Sicknesse'. However, it still did not explain why Oppenheimer picked the name Trinity. Groves concluded that there was another, better known devotional poem by Donne that began: 'Batter my heart, three person'd God.'

This is the fourteenth of Donne's *Holy Sonnets* and explores the theme of a destruction that might also redeem.

Oppenheimer, like many of those who worked with him, still thought this most deadly weapon might, once and for all, put an end to war.

Ground Zero

The army leased the ranch belonging to David McDonald in the middle of the Jornada site and converted it into a military police station and field laboratory, thoroughly vacuumed to make it a makeshift clean room and with its windows sealed with black electrical tape. Nearly two miles to the northwest, Bainbridge marked out the spot for Ground Zero.

Three concrete-roofed observation bunkers with bullet-proof glass portholes were dug 10,000 yards north, west and south of Ground Zero. From there, the test would be controlled and key aspects of the explosion would be filmed and measured. Scientists wanted to determine the symmetry of the implosion and the amount of energy released. They also wanted to get estimates of the damage that the bomb would cause and study the behaviour of the resulting fireball.

The biggest concern was the radioactivity the test device would release. It was hoped that favourable meteorological conditions would carry the radioactivity into the upper atmosphere. As they were proposing to do the test in the middle of the thunderstorm season, the army stood ready to evacuate the people in surrounding areas.

Two towers were built. One was 800 yards south of Ground Zero. Made of heavy wooden beams, it was 20 feet high, topped with a broad platform like an outdoor dance floor. One day, the contractors returned to find that it had disappeared. Bainbridge had loaded the platform with canisters of radioactive waste from Hanford and surrounded it with 100 tons of high explosives. Before dawn on 7 May, he detonated the largest chemical explosion ever set off to test the instruments and procedures in a practice firing.

The tower at Ground Zero had been prefabricated in steel and was shipped in sections to the Trinity site, where concrete footings had been sunk 20 feet into the rocky desert floor. The four feet were 35 feet apart and the tower rose 100 feet above the ground. Near the top was a platform with a removable centre section and corrugated iron sheets on three sides. The open side faced the camera bunker to the west. Above the platform was a $20,000 electrically driven heavy-duty winch.

Last-minute problems

Oppenheimer insisted on an exact copy of the gadget without a fissionable core. This left Kistiakowsky short of high-quality lens castings. X-rays showed that they had tiny air pockets trapped inside the explosives. He got hold of a dental drill and spent most of the night drilling into the faulty castings to reach the air cavities. Then he poured molten explosive slurry into the holes to fill the cavities.

Kistiakowsky was blasé about the danger. 'You don't worry about it,' he said. 'I mean, if 50 pounds of explosives goes in your lap, you won't know it.'

The castings were then checked for further damage. Two globes were prepared – one for the test firing and one for the Trinity assembly. For the gadget itself, one cast had been left out so that the core could be positioned inside the tamper.

By then, two small plutonium hemispheres had been cast. They had been plated with nickel to prevent corrosion and absorb harmful alpha particles. But plating solution trapped under the skin began to blister, spoiling the fit. Filing off the blisters completely would have exposed the plutonium, so the metallurgists improvised, grinding part way through the blisters and smoothing the surface with gold foil to ensure a snug fit.

Final assembly

On 12 July, the plutonium core was taken to the test area in an army sedan. The non-nuclear components of the bomb left for the test site at 12:01am on Friday the 13th. The idea was to put a 'reverse English' on the ill-luck that day was supposed to augur. As they rode through Santa Fe in the small hours, the convoy sounded a siren. The army did not want to risk some late-night drunken driver speeding out of a side street into a truck full of high explosives.

Final assembly of the gadget took place in the McDonald ranch house. Before it began, Bacher asked for a receipt from the army. As Los Alamos was technically part of the University of California, he did not want the university to be liable for the several million dollars-worth of plutonium they were about to vaporize.

Then the team nestled the beryllium-polonium neutron initiator that would trigger the explosion between the two hemispheres of plutonium. These were hot to the touch due to the alpha particles given off. The nickel-skinned ball was then placed inside a cylinder of U-238 tamper. The core was then driven out to Ground Zero, where it arrived at 3.18pm.

The five-foot sphere of high explosives had arrived that morning. This was wrapped around a hollow globe of U-238. At 1pm, the winch was used to hoist the 2 ton ball of high explosives from the back of the truck and lower it onto a skid.

'We were scared to death that we would drop it,' said Norris Bradbury, the navy physicist in charge of the assembly, 'because we did not trust the hoist and it was the only bomb immediately available. It wasn't that we were afraid of setting it off, but we might damage it in some way.'

Tight fit

A white tent was erected over the assembly, ready for the cylindrical plug containing the plutonium spheres and the initiator to be slid into place in the centre of the ball of tamper inside the explosives.

'Imagine our consternation when, as we started to assemble the plug in the hole, deep down in the centre of the high-explosive shell, it would not enter,' Boyce McDaniel, one of

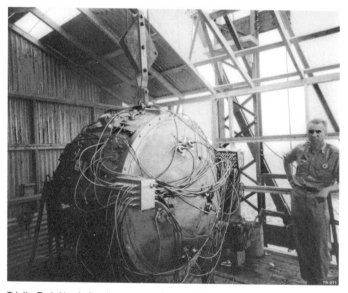

Trinity Test: Norris Bradbury, group leader for bomb assembly, stands next to the partially assembled Gadget atop the test tower. Later, he became the director of Los Alamos, after the departure of Oppenheimer.

the assembly team, said. 'Dismayed, we halted our efforts in order not to damage the pieces, and stopped to think about it. Could we have made a mistake?'

To maximize the density of uranium in the assembly, the clearance between the plug and the spherical shell had been reduced to a few thousandths of an inch. Three sets of the plugs and tamper spheres had been made back in Los Alamos. In the haste of their construction, not all the plugs fitted into all the holes. Surely they could not have brought the wrong ones.

Then Bacher realized what had happened. In the heat of the ranch house, the plug had expanded, while the tamper sphere, insulated by the explosives wrapped around it, was still cool from Los Alamos. The team left the metal of the plug and the sphere in contact and took a break. Later, when they checked the assembly again, the temperature had equalized and the plug slid smoothly into place. That evening, the last block of explosive was Scotch-taped into place. The detonators were installed the following day.

At 8am on 15 July, the device was hoisted up the firing tower, stopping at 15 feet for a team of GIs to stack army-issue mattresses under it in case it should fall. While this was being done, news came that measurements from the test-firing indicated that Trinity would fail. Everybody blamed Kistiakowsky, but he was adamant.

'Oppenheimer became so emotional that I offered him a month's salary against ten dollars that our implosion charges would work,' he said.

While this was going on, Little Boy, the uranium bomb with its gun mechanism, was leaving Los Alamos for Kirtland Air Force Base in Albuquerque. From there it would be flown to San Francisco, where it would be loaded on to the USS *Indianapolis* and padlocked to the deck in an anonymous 15 foot crate for shipment to Tinian.

Then came good news. After a night analysing the data from the test-firing, Hans Bethe called to say that something was wrong with the instruments and even a perfect implosion would have registered as a dud.

'So I became acceptable to local high society,' said Kistiakowsky.

Delayed by rain

Groves, Bush, Conant, Lawrence, Farrell, Bethe, Teller and Chadwick, head of the British contingent at Los Alamos and discoverer of the neutron, arrived in the test area. It was pouring with rain.

In the control bunker 5.7 miles to the south, Groves and Oppenheimer discussed what to do if the weather did not break in time for the test scheduled at 4am. At 3.30am they pushed the time back to 5.30, when the meteorologist Jack M. Hubbard forecast there would be a break in the weather.

'You'd better be right on this, or I will hang you,' Groves told Hubbard before calling the governor of New Mexico, getting him out of bed to warn him that he might have to declare martial law.

Fermi spent the wait annoying Groves.

'He suddenly offered to take wagers from his fellow scientists on whether or not the bomb would ignite the atmosphere, and if so, whether it would merely destroy New Mexico or destroy the world,' Groves recalled. 'He also said that after all it wouldn't make any difference whether the bomb went off or not because it would still have been a well worthwhile scientific experiment. For if it did fail to go off, we would have proved that an atomic explosion was not possible.'

At 4am the rain stopped. Kistiakowsky and his team armed the device shortly after 5am and retreated to the control bunker. Their final task was to switch on a string of lights on the ground that would serve as an 'aiming point'. The air force wanted to know what the effect of the blast would be on a B-29 bomber 30,000 feet up and some miles away.

In case of an accident, Groves left Oppenheimer in the control bunkers and joined Bush and Conant at base camp another 5 miles to the south. There they picked up the countdown by FM radio. Those in shelters heard it over the PA system.

Some of the scientists were with a party of onlookers 20 miles away on Compania Hill. There, Teller said, 'We were told to lie down on the sand, turn our faces away from the blast and bury our heads in our arms. No one complied. We were determined to look the beast in the eye.'

However, though it was not yet dawn, they smothered their faces with suntan lotion. Teller himself wore a pair of dark glasses and heavy gloves and pressed a welder's glass to his face.

Dawn of the atomic age

At precisely 5:30am on Monday, 16 July 1945, the atomic age began. As the firing circuit closed, 32 detonators fired around the outside of the high-explosive shell. The shockwave produced hit the tamper, squeezing and liquefying it. The plutonium sphere inside shrank to the size of an eyeball. In the centre, polonium alphas kicked neutrons from the beryllium – one, two, maybe as many as nine of them. This was enough to start a chain reaction in the plutonium. It went through 80 generations in millionths of a second, generating millions of degrees of heat and millions of pounds of pressure.

The X-rays given off super-heated the air, generating another shock wave. The explosion vaporized the tower and

Rare government image of J. Robert Oppenheimer (in light coloured hat with foot on tower rubble), General Leslie Groves (in military dress to Oppenheimer's left), and others at the ground zero site of the Trinity test after the bombing of Hiroshima and Nagasaki.

turned the asphalt around the base into green sand. The bomb released approximately 18.6 kilotons of power, and the New Mexico sky was suddenly brighter than many suns.

Some observers suffered temporary blindness even though they looked at the brilliant light through smoked glass. Seconds after the explosion came a huge blast, sending searing heat across the desert and knocking some observers to the ground. A steel container weighing more than 200 tons, standing half a mile from Ground Zero, was knocked over.

As the orange and yellow fireball stretched up and spread, a second column, narrower than the first, rose and flattened into a mushroom shape, giving the atomic age a visual image that has become the very symbol of power and awesome destruction.

Oppenheimer said: 'We waited until the blast had passed,

walked out of the shelter and then it was extremely solemn. A few people laughed, a few people cried. I remembered the line from the Hindu scripture the *Bhagavad-Gita*: Vishnu is trying to persuade the Prince that he could do his duty and to impress him takes on his multi-armed form and says, "Now I am become Death, the destroyers of worlds." I suppose we all thought that, one way or another.'

Later he recalled that the experience brought to his mind the legend of Prometheus, punished by Zeus for giving man fire. He also thought fleetingly of Alfred Nobel's vain hope that his discovery of dynamite would end wars.

At base camp, Bush, Conant and Groves shook hands. Hubbard heard Groves say: 'My faith in the human mind has been somewhat restored.'

In the sweepstake, Rabi had put his money on 18 kilotons and swept the pot. He broke out a bottle of whiskey and everyone had a swig.

The terrifying destructive power of atomic weapons and the uses to which they might be put were to haunt many of the scientists from the Manhattan Project for the rest of their lives. But for the moment, the success of the Trinity test meant that a second type of atomic bomb could be readied for use against Japan. Oppenheimer and Groves wrote a report for Stimson who was now in Potsdam. Along with Little Boy, the untested uranium gun model Fat Man, a plutonium implosion device similar to that detonated at Trinity, now figured in American Far Eastern strategy.

Chapter Ten
The Potsdam Declaration

President Truman, Secretary of State Byrnes, Secretary of War Stimson and the American contingent to the conference of the Big Three – the US, the UK and the USSR – had arrived in Berlin on 15 July 1945. They spent most of the next two days discussing how to persuade the Soviet Union to declare war on Japan and grappling with the wording of the surrender document to be presented to the Japanese. The sticking point was the term 'unconditional'. It was clear that the Japanese would fight on rather than accept terms that would remove the Imperial House or demean the nation's warrior tradition. However, the American policy-makers feared that anything less than a democratic political system and total demilitarization would lead to Japanese aggression in the future. Much effort went into finding the precise formula that would satisfy American public opinion regarding the losses suffered in the Pacific, without incurring more in a costly invasion of the Japanese mainland.

It was clear to the Japanese that the war was lost. In an attempt to achieve surrender with honour, Emperor Hirohito had instructed his ministers to open negotiations with Russia. The US intercepted and decoded messages between Tokyo and

British Prime Minister Winston Churchill (left), President Harry S. Truman (centre) and Soviet leader Josef Stalin in the garden of Cecilienhof Palace before meeting for the Potsdam Conference in Potsdam, Germany, 1945.

Moscow that made it unmistakably clear that the Japanese were searching for an alternative to unconditional surrender.

However, the Russians refused to help when the Japanese put out peace feelers. Forty years before, Japan had soundly beaten Russia in the Russo-Japanese War, sinking two Russian fleets and putting an end to Russian expansion in the east. They had clashed again at the Battle of Nomonhan in Mongolia in the summer of 1939, when Japan's attempt to invade Siberia was thwarted, weeks before Hitler's invasion of Poland started World War II. Now, with the imminent defeat of the Japanese, Stalin hoped to make territorial gains.

News of Trinity

Stalin arrived in Berlin a day late, leaving Stimson on 16 July to mull over questions of the post-war administration and military situation in the Far East. After sending Truman and Byrnes a memorandum advocating sending an early warning to Japan of an atomic attack and setting out a bargaining strategy to get Russia into the Pacific war, Stimson received a cable from George L. Harrison, his special consultant in Washington. It read: 'Operated on this morning. Diagnosis not yet complete but results seem satisfactory and already exceed expectations. Local press release necessary as interest extends great distance. Dr Groves pleased. He returns tomorrow. I will keep you posted.'

Stimson immediately informed Truman and Byrnes that the Trinity test had been successful. The next day Stimson told Churchill about the test. The prime minister expressed great delight and argued forcefully against informing the Russians, though he later relented. On 18 July, while debate continued over the wording of the surrender message, focusing on whether or not to guarantee the place of the emperor, Stimson received a second cable from Harrison: 'Doctor has just returned most enthusiastic and confident that the little boy is as husky as his big brother. The light in his eyes discernible from here to Highhold and I could have heard his screams from here to my farm.'

Highhold was Stimson's estate on Long Island, 250 miles from Washington, while Harrison's farm was 50 miles outside the capital. In other words, Groves thought that the plutonium weapon would be as powerful as the uranium device and that the flash from the Trinity test could be seen 250 miles away and the noise heard for 50 miles. Initial measurements taken at the site suggested that Trinity had an explosive power in excess of 5,000 tons of TNT; the 18.6 kilotons had yet to be confirmed. Truman went back to the bargaining table with a new card in his hand.

Further information on the Trinity test arrived on 21 July in the form of a long report from Groves. Los Alamos scientists now agreed that the blast had been the equivalent of 15,000–20,000 tons of TNT, higher than anyone had predicted. Groves reported that window panes had shattered 125 miles away, that the fireball was brighter than several suns at midday and that the steel tower had been completely vaporized. Though he had previously thought the Pentagon was impregnable, Groves said that he did not consider it safe from atomic attack.

Stimson informed Marshall, then read the entire report to Truman and Byrnes. Stimson recorded that Truman was 'tremendously pepped up' and that the document gave him 'an entirely new feeling of confidence'. The next day, Stimson was informed that the uranium bomb would be ready in early August and discussed Groves's report at great length with Churchill. The British prime minister was elated. He had given his consent for the bomb to be used against Japan as early as 4 July, before the test in New Mexico had even taken place. He later gave his reasons for doing so: 'To avert a vast, indefinite butchery, to bring the war to an end, to give peace to the world, to lay healing hands upon its tortured peoples by a manifestation of overwhelming power at the cost of a few explosions, seemed, after all our toils and perils, the miracle of development.' According to Groves, 'Prime Minister Churchill was probably the best friend that the Manhattan Project ever had.'

After hearing Groves's report, Churchill said that he now understood why Truman had been so forceful with Stalin the previous day, especially in his opposition to Russian designs on Eastern Europe and Germany. Churchill then told Truman that the bomb could lead to Japanese surrender without an invasion and eliminate the necessity for Soviet military help. He recommended that the president continue to take a hard line with Stalin. Truman and his advisors shared Churchill's views. The success of the Trinity test stiffened Truman's resolve, and he refused to accede to Stalin's new demands for concessions in Turkey and the Mediterranean.

On 24 July Stimson met with Truman. He told the president that Marshall no longer saw any need for Russian help and briefed him on the latest S-1 situation. The uranium bomb might be ready as early as 1 August and certainly by 10 August. The plutonium weapon would be available by 6 August.

Truman informs Stalin

British and American planning of an invasion of Japan continued, with 1 November as its D-Day. At a meeting with British and American military strategists at Potsdam, the Soviets reported that their troops were moving into the Far East and would be ready to enter the war in the middle of August. They would drive the Japanese out of Manchuria and withdraw at the end of hostilities. This allowed Truman to calm his Chinese ally's fears, assuring the Chinese foreign minister that Russia's intentions in the Far East were benevolent.

On the evening of 24 July, Truman left his translator behind, as Stalin spoke excellent English, learned during his stay in London before World War I. 'I casually mentioned to Stalin that we had a new weapon of unusual destructive force,' said Truman. 'The Russian premier showed no special interest. All he said was that he was glad to hear it and hoped we would make "good use of it against the Japanese".'

The reason for Stalin's composure became clear later when it was learned that Russian intelligence had been receiving information about the Manhattan Project from Klaus Fuchs and other agents since it began in the summer of 1942.

The Potsdam Proclamation

A directive, written by Groves and issued by Stimson and Marshall on 25 July, ordered the Army Air Force's 509th Composite Group to attack Hiroshima, Kokura, Niigata, or Nagasaki 'after about' 3 August, or as soon as weather permitted. The 509th was ready. Tests with dummies had been conducted successfully. Operation Bronx, which brought the gun and U-235 projectile to Tinian aboard the USS *Indianapolis*, was complete. Other parts were carried on board five C-54 Skymasters, while three B-29s carried the components of
Fat Man.

On 26 July the Potsdam Proclamation demanding Japan's surrender was issued. It said:

1. We – the President of the United States, the President of the National Government of the Republic of China, and the Prime Minister of Great Britain, representing the hundreds of millions of our countrymen, have conferred and agree that Japan shall be given an opportunity to end this war.
2. The prodigious land, sea and air forces of the United States, the British Empire and of China, many times reinforced by their armies and air fleets from the west, are poised to strike the final blows upon Japan. This military power is sustained and inspired by the determination of all the Allied Nations to prosecute the war against Japan until she ceases to resist.
3. The result of the futile and senseless German resistance to the might of the aroused free peoples of the world stands forth in awful clarity as an example to the people of Japan. The might that now converges on Japan is immeasurably greater than that which, when applied to the resisting Nazis, necessarily laid waste to the lands, the industry and

the method of life of the whole German people. The full application of our military power, backed by our resolve, will mean the inevitable and complete destruction of the Japanese armed forces and just as inevitably the utter devastation of the Japanese homeland.

4. The time has come for Japan to decide whether she will continue to be controlled by those self-willed militaristic advisers whose unintelligent calculations have brought the Empire of Japan to the threshold of annihilation, or whether she will follow the path of reason.

5. Following are our terms. We will not deviate from them. There are no alternatives. We shall brook no delay.

6. There must be eliminated for all time the authority and influence of those who have deceived and misled the people of Japan into embarking on world conquest, for we insist that a new order of peace, security and justice will be impossible until irresponsible militarism is driven from the world.

7. Until such a new order is established and until there is convincing proof that Japan's war-making power is destroyed, points in Japanese territory to be designated by the Allies shall be occupied to secure the achievement of the basic objectives we are here setting forth.

8. The terms of the Cairo Declaration shall be carried out and Japanese sovereignty shall be limited to the islands of Honshu, Hokkaido, Kyushu, Shikoku and such minor islands as we determine.

9. The Japanese military forces, after being completely disarmed, shall be permitted to return to their homes with the opportunity to lead peaceful and productive lives.

10. We do not intend that the Japanese shall be enslaved as a race or destroyed as a nation, but stern justice shall be meted out to all war criminals, including those who have visited cruelties upon our prisoners. The Japanese

Government shall remove all obstacles to the revival and strengthening of democratic tendencies among the Japanese people. Freedom of speech, of religion, and of thought, as well as respect for the fundamental human rights shall be established.

11. Japan shall be permitted to maintain such industries as will sustain her economy and permit the exaction of just reparations in kind, but not those which would enable her to re-arm for war. To this end, access to, as distinguished from control of, raw materials shall be permitted. Eventual Japanese participation in world trade relations shall be permitted.

12. The occupying forces of the Allies shall be withdrawn from Japan as soon as these objectives have been accomplished and there has been established in accordance with the freely expressed will of the Japanese people a peacefully inclined and responsible government.

13. We call upon the government of Japan to proclaim now the unconditional surrender of all Japanese armed forces, and to provide proper and adequate assurances of their good faith in such action. The alternative for Japan is prompt and utter destruction.

The president of China was Chiang Kai-Shek, later the president of Nationalist China, confined to the island of Taiwan, and the prime minister of Great Britain was then Clement Attlee, as Winston Churchill had just lost the election. The Cairo Declaration had called for Japan's surrender in 1943 and for the return of all the land the Japanese had occupied. The Soviets were not informed of the wording of the Potsdam Proclamation in advance as they were not at war with Japan, and while the proclamation threatened the 'prompt and utter destruction' it did not mention that the Allies now had the weapon to make good that threat. Although the USAAF had dropped more than 63 million leaflets warning Japanese civilians of air-raids, they were largely disbelieved, and it was decided not to drop a special leaflet before unleashing the atomic bomb as it was thought that it would reduce the psychological impact.

The Potsdam Proclamation left the emperor's status unclear by making no reference to the royal house. Cables between Tokyo and Moscow, again intercepted by American intelligence, revealed that the Japanese wanted to surrender but felt they could not accept the terms offered in the Potsdam Proclamation.

Weighting destruction in the balance

The Japanese had an army of two million men on the home islands. There were some 5300 aircraft ready to carry out *kamikaze* attacks and around 3300 suicide boats were being packed with explosives to greet a seaborne invasion. Though there was little fuel to send them into action, the Japanese thought that they could inflict sufficient casualties on the Americans to force them to the negotiating table.

Under the invasion plans drawn up by Marshall, 190,000 American troops were ready to land on Japan's most southerly island of Kyushu on 1 November. The invasion of the main island, Honshu, would follow five months later. As many as five million troops would be used. The landings on Kyushu alone, it was estimated, would cost 69,000 American casualties. The Allies had already witnessed fanatical resistance from the Japanese all the way across the Pacific – as well as from Germans when forced back into their homeland. They were expecting to lose up to half a million men in the invasion of Japan, maybe more. Even on Okinawa the Japanese had inflicted 35 per cent casualties. This was too high a price to pay.

A declaration of war by the Soviet Union might have convinced Japan to surrender, but the price tag would have been that Stalin would expect to share in the post-war administration of Japan. This would have jeopardized American plans in the Far East.

By then, a blockade by Allied submarines and air-dropped mines had brought the Japanese economy to a standstill. The home islands could not produce enough food to support the population. Nevertheless, the continued blockade of Japan combined with conventional bombing was rejected as too time-consuming and an invasion of the islands as too costly. And few believed that a demonstration of the atomic bomb in some remote and uninhabited spot would convince the Japanese to give up.

Consequently, American policy-makers concluded that the atomic bomb must be used. Hiroshima was placed first on the list, thought to be the only prime target city with no prisoner-of-war camps in the vicinity. As the final touches were put on the message Truman would issue after the attack, word came that the first bomb could be dropped as early as 1 August – but poor weather led to several days' delay.

USS *Indianapolis*

After delivering the gun assembly of Little Boy to Tinian, the USS *Indianapolis* was heading for the Philippines for training when it was spotted by Japanese submarine I-58 shortly before midnight on Sunday, 29 July. The submarine rapidly submerged and fired a salvo of six torpedoes in the fan formation.

The captain, Lieutenant Commander Mochitsura Hashimoto, said: 'I took a quick look through the periscope, but there was nothing else in sight. Bringing the boat on to a course parallel with the enemy, we waited anxiously. Every minute seemed an age. Then on the starboard side of the enemy by the forward turret, and then by the after turret, there rose columns of water, to be followed immediately by flashes of bright red flame. Then another column of water rose from alongside Number 1 turret and seemed to envelop the whole ship. 'A hit, a hit!' I shouted as each torpedo struck home, and the crew danced around with joy . . . Soon came the sound of a heavy explosion, far greater than that of the actual hits. Three more heavy explosions followed in quick succession, then six more.' The torpedoes and the explosion of the ammunition and aviation fuel it was carrying ripped off the cruiser's bow and destroyed its power centre so no distress signal could be sent. The ship ploughed on, scooping water into its gaping hull.

Men with terrible burns were thrown into the salt water. Those attempting to walk down the hull were sliced up by the spinning propellers. As the stern rose 100 feet in the air and the ship went down, screams were heard from within.

Of the 1196 men on board, some 850 escaped. They were left floating in the darkness without lifeboats in 12 foot swells. The next day, survivors were blinded and burnt by the glare of the sun. Then the sharks came. Monday and Tuesday passed with no fresh water. Those who drank seawater grew manic and thrashed about violently before they became comatose and drowned.

The sharks moved in again for a fresh meal on Wednesday. Hallucinating, one swimmer set off for an island he thought he saw. Another pursued a ghost ship. Yet another swam down to the fountains of fresh water he had glimpsed deep beneath the sea.

Some survivors sank as their kapok lifejackets became waterlogged, dragging them to their deaths. Meanwhile, the ship had not even been missed. On Thursday the men in the water were spotted by a navy plane. Food, water and survival gear was dropped. Then, after 84 hours in the water, 318 men were rescued. One of them was the ship's captain, Charles Butler McVay III. Though 350 US Navy ships were lost in combat in World War II, McVay was the only captain to be court-martialled, convicted of 'hazarding his ship by failing to zigzag'. In 2001, some 33 years after his death, he was exonerated by President Clinton. However, there is no mechanism to overturn the verdict of a court martial.

Chapter Eleven
The Quick and the Dead

General Carl A. Spaatz was in Washington, DC, on his way to take command of the US Army Strategic Air Forces in the Pacific when he was told of the atomic bomb and Truman's decision. He refused to drop such weapons on a purely verbal order and was given written orders that the 509th Group would deliver the first bomb as soon after 3 August as weather permitted.

Poor weather held off the attack until 6 August. At 2.45am that day, a B-29, named 'Enola Gay' by pilot Paul Tibbets after his mother, clawed its way into the sky. The 9000-pound Little Boy had put the plane 8 tons over its normal bombing weight and there was a danger that the plane would crash on take-off. Consequently, the bomb was not armed. Deke Parsons was on board. He would arm the bomb once airborne on the way to Hiroshima, an important military and communications centre with a population of nearly 300,000. This was designated as the first target as it was the home of the Japanese 2nd Army, which was responsible for the defence of the southwest sector of the homeland. It was this army that any invading force would be up against.

Located in the deltas of south-western Honshu Island facing

Pilot Paul Tibbets waves from the Enola Gay. *The B-29 dropped the atomic bomb on the Japanese city of Hiroshima.*

the Inland Sea, Hiroshima was 1500 miles away. Heading northwards, Tibbets flew at low altitude on automatic pilot before climbing to 31,000 feet as they neared the target area.

At 7.15am Major Claude Eatherly, in a B-29 over Hiroshima acting as a weather-scout, signalled that the skies over the city were open. When he left, the all-clear was sounded in the city below. Until then Hiroshima had almost completely escaped bombing, so few people took any notice when two more B-29s flying at 31,600 feet appeared at 8.06. They were so high that no air-raid alarm was sounded as it seemed they would simply over-fly the city.

The attack

As the observation and photography escorts fell back, the Enola Gay dropped Little Boy and then turned sharply away. A second plane dropped a parachute carrying a package of scientific instruments. Seventeen seconds after 8.15am, the bomb exploded just below 1900 feet over the most built-up part of the city and directly over a parade field where the Japanese 2nd Army was doing early morning callisthenics.

There was a blind flash of bluish-white light. This was followed by a searing heat. Then there was a roar a thousand times louder than thunder and the ground shook. The blast, equivalent to 17,000 tons of TNT, started a firestorm. Some 4.7 square miles of the city were completely flattened and 60,000 of the 90,000 buildings within 9½ square miles were destroyed or badly damaged. Everything in a 2 mile radius of the explosion's epicentre was vaporized.

Although it was already 11½ miles away, the Enola Gay was rocked by the blast. At first Tibbets thought he was taking flak. After a second shockwave hit the plane, the crew looked back at Hiroshima.

'The city was hidden by that awful cloud, boiling up, mushrooming, terrible and incredibly tall,' Tibbets recalled.

Seeing the inferno, tail gunner Sergeant George Caron exclaimed: 'My God, what have we done?'

Later he described the deadly mushroom cloud he saw forming behind him: 'It's like a mass of bubbling molasses. The

The huge mushroom-shaped cloud that rose over Hiroshima following the explosion of the first atomic bomb.

mushroom is spreading out. It's maybe a mile or two wide and half a mile high. It's growing up and up. It's nearly level with us and climbing. It's very black but there is a purplish tint to the cloud. The base of the mushroom looks like a heavy under-cast that is shot through with flames.'

The dead

It is not known how many of the population perished in Hiroshima. The names of 61,443 people are inscribed on the cenotaph that sits at ground zero, directly under the point where the bomb exploded. However, the US Strategic Bombing Survey estimated that there were 139,402 casualties, including 71,379 known dead and missing presumed dead. These included 20 American airmen held as PoWs.

More than 20,000 of the dead were school children. There were also 68,023 injured, 19,691 seriously. Only later did the devastating effects of radiation make themselves felt. By the end of 1945, the Hiroshima death toll rose to 140,000 as radiation sickness deaths mounted. Five years later the total reached 200,000.

Reconnaissance view of the Japanese Army base at Hiroshima, which was the first enemy target to feel the weight of the new Atomic bomb.

The bomb caused total devastation for 5 square miles, with almost all of the buildings in the city either destroyed or damaged. The shape of warfare had been changed forever. Now no distinction at all could be made between military and civilian targets. All were swept to their deaths by a deadly nuclear wind, just as the scientists, military and politicians involved knew they would be. Ironically, the city's munitions factories, which were on the outskirts, survived.

The fate of survivors

One middle school student in Hiroshima said: 'I'll never forget that day. After we finished our morning greetings in the schoolyard, we were waiting in the classroom. Suddenly a friend by the window shouted "B-29!" At the same instant, a flash pierced my eyes. The entire building collapsed at once and we were trapped underneath. I don't know how long I remained unconscious.

'When I came to, I couldn't move my body. Cuts on my face and hands throbbed with pain. My front teeth were broken and my shirt was soaked in blood. As I crawled along, encouraging myself, I somehow managed to poke my head out of the wreckage. The school that should have appeared before my eyes was nowhere to be seen. It had vanished and only smouldering ruins remained.

'Beyond the school towards the centre of town, all I could see was a sea of flames. I was so terrified I couldn't stop shaking. Moving my body a little at a time, I was finally able to work free of the collapsed structure. Making sure to head upwind to escape the fires, I made my way staggering haphazardly through the rubble of the city.'

Fourteen-year-old Akihiro Takahashi was attending

assembly at Hiroshima Municipal Junior High School, nearly a mile from the centre of the blast.

'We were about to form lines facing the front,' Akihiro said. 'We saw a B-29 approaching and about to fly over us. All of us were looking up at the sky, pointing out the aircraft. Then the teachers came out from the school building and the class leaders gave the command to fall in. Our faces were all shifted from the direction of the sky to that of the platform.

'That was the moment when the blast came. And then the tremendous noise came and we were left in the dark. I couldn't see anything at the moment of explosion . . . We had been blown by the blast. Of course, I couldn't realize this until the

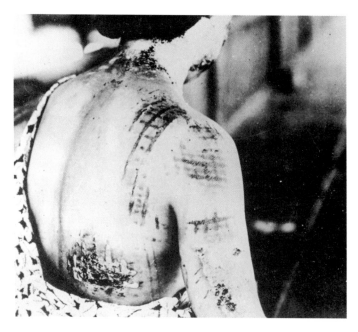

A Japanese woman's severe burns caused by the bombing of Hiroshima.

darkness disappeared. I was actually blown about 10 metres. My friends were all marked down on the ground by the blast. Everything collapsed for as far as I could see. I felt the city of Hiroshima had disappeared all of a sudden. Then I looked at myself and found my clothes had turned into rags due to the heat.

'I was probably burned at the back of the head, on my back, on both arms and both legs. My skin was peeling and hanging. Automatically I began to walk, heading west because that was the direction of my home. After a while, I noticed somebody calling my name. I looked around and found a friend of mine who lived in my town and was studying at the same school. His name was Yamamoto. He was badly burnt just like myself.

'We walked towards the river. And on the way we saw many victims. I saw a man whose skin was completely peeled off the upper half of his body and a woman whose eyeballs were sticking out. Her whole body was bleeding. A mother and her baby were lying with their skin completely peeled off. We desperately made our way crawling. And finally we reached the riverbank. At the same moment, a fire broke out. We made a narrow escape from the fire. If we had been slower by even one second, we would have been killed by the fire.

'Fire was blowing into the sky, becoming four or even five metres high. There was a small wooden bridge left, which had not been destroyed by the blast. I went over to the other side of the river using that bridge. But Yamamoto was not with me any more. He was lost somewhere. I remember I crossed the river by myself and on the other side, I plunged myself into the water three times. The heat was tremendous. And I felt like my body was burning all over. For my burning body the cold water of the river was as precious as a treasure.

'Then I left the river, and I walked along the railroad tracks in the direction of my home. On the way, I ran into another friend of mine, Tokujiro Hatta. I wondered why the soles of his feet were badly burnt. It was unthinkable to get burned there. But it was undeniable fact the soles were peeling and red muscle was exposed. Even though I myself was terribly burnt, I could not go home ignoring him. I made him crawl using his arms and knees. Next, I made him stand on his heels and I supported him. We walked heading toward my home repeating the two methods. When we were resting because we were so exhausted, I found my grandfather's brother and his wife, in other words, great uncle and great aunt, coming toward us. That was quite a coincidence. As you know, we have a proverb about meeting Buddha in Hell. My encounter with my relatives at that time was just like that. They seem to be the Buddha to me wandering in the living hell.'

Telling the world

Within hours of the attack, radio stations began broadcasting a prepared statement from President Harry Truman informing the American public that the United States had dropped an entirely new type of bomb on the Japanese city of Hiroshima – an atomic bomb with more power than 15,000 tons of TNT. Truman warned that if Japan still refused to surrender unconditionally as demanded by the Potsdam Proclamation of 26 July, the United States would attack additional targets with equally devastating results.

News of the destruction of Hiroshima was not carried in the Japanese newspapers. It was said that it had come under attack by incendiaries. No surrender was forthcoming. Indeed, in Hiroshima, survivors were buoyed by rumours that Japan had retaliated, using 'the same mysterious weapon' against major cities in California, snatching victory from the jaws of defeat.

Two days later, on 8 August, the Soviet Union declared war

on Japan and attacked Japanese forces in Manchuria, ending American hopes that the war would end before Russian entry into the Pacific theatre. By the end of the war, the Red Army had seized the northern part of Korea and taken more than 2.7 million Japanese prisoners. Fewer than half a million returned home.

Factional struggles and communications problems prevented Japan from meeting Allied terms in the immediate aftermath of Hiroshima. Having received no reply to the Potsdam Declaration, conventional bombing raids on additional Japanese cities continued as scheduled. Then, on 9 August, a second atomic attack was ordered.

Nagasaki

At 3.49am on 9 August 1945, the B-29 'Bockscar' piloted by Major Charles W. Sweeney took off from Tinian, carrying the 4½ tons of Fat Man. This was an altogether more hazardous procedure as the plutonium bomb had to be armed before take-off. Kokura with its enormous army arsenal was the primary target, with the harbour at Nagasaki with its four large Mitsubishi

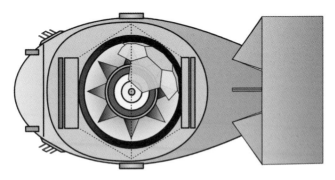

Fat man with its 6-kg plutonium core.

Fat Man is assembled at Tinian air base ready for its fatal flight.

factories involved in war production the secondary; the torpedoes used at Pearl Harbor had been made there. The Enola Gay was also airborne that day, this time as a reconnaissance plane.

A storm brewing over the Pacific delayed the aircraft carrying the British observers. While Bockscar waited at the rendezvous point, the clouds closed in over Kokura. Sweeney made three passes over the target, encountering some flak, then decided to head for Nagasaki. It too was obscured by cloud cover and Bockscar was running low on fuel. There was only enough for a single bombing run, so a radar drop was authorized, but at the last moment a hole opened in the clouds, allowing visual targeting at 29,000 feet.

At 11.02am, Fat Man was dropped 3 miles from the designated dropping point, but directly over the city's industrial heart. The plane then veered off and headed to Okinawa for an emergency landing with just a few gallons of fuel left.

As the dropping of an atomic bomb on Hiroshima had not been reported in the Japanese papers, no one was prepared. There had been an air raid alert at 07.48am but only 400 or so people were in the shelters, which were just big enough for around a third of Nagasaki's 195,290 residents.

Fat Man exploded 1650 feet above the slopes of the city with a force of 21,000 tons of TNT. The surrounding hills concentrated the blast, but protected the rest of the city. Only 1.45 square miles were completely destroyed. There was no firestorm and little panic, but 68 per cent of the industrial capacity of the city was destroyed.

The official Japanese casualty figures record 23,753 killed, 1,927 missing and 23,345 injured. Again, the US Strategic Bombing Survey put the figures higher, with more than 35,000 dead and more injured. By January 1946, 70,000 people had died in Nagasaki. The total eventually reached 140,000, with a death rate similar to that of Hiroshima.

A flash of light

Again, the effects on the victims on the ground were horrific. Sakue Shimohira was just six years old when the Pacific war began. There was little to eat and she had to go to school barefoot as she had no shoes. The government slogan at the time was 'Forget your wishes until we've won.'

On the morning of 9 August, the air-raid sirens sounded early and the children rushed to their regular dugout around 875 yards from what would be the epicentre of the blast. They hid in the dark hole until they heard a voice saying: 'Air-raid warning lifted, air-raid warning lifted.' Some of the children rushed outside, but Sakue and her sisters stayed in the shelter.

'That was the moment it happened,' she said. 'There was a flash of light, and the very second that it appeared as though the hole was illuminated from corner to corner, a violent gust of wind blew in. We were blown off our feet, dashed against the rocks, and I fainted. Somebody slapped my head, and I regained my senses.'

When she came round, she was shocked. The air-raid shelter, which should have been empty, was full of people with charred bodies; people with ripped flesh, covered in blood; people whose eyeballs had burst out of their sockets; people whose burns had swollen their bodies by two or three times. Everywhere people were wailing, 'Give me some water, help me!'

'I was scared, paralysed with fear and unable to move,' said Sakue. 'All I could do was scream, "Mummy, help me!"'

Her younger sister had been sent flying by the blast, and Sakue had no idea what had happened to her friends. Her elder sister's child had also been swept away. Eventually the three of them were reunited and they huddled together, screaming for help. But no help came.

'We could hear a voice crying, "Who's there? Somebody kill me!"' said Sakue. 'We looked and saw one of my older friends, Sakurai, sprawled on the ground. His stomach was burst and his intestines were hanging out.'

The shelter stank of charred corpses, and they vomited as they waited for aid. Finally, they heard a voice outside asking, 'Is there anyone alive in there?'

They yelled for help. Sakue's foster father had come to rescue them, and got them out.

'Again I was shocked,' said Sakue. 'Not a single house was left standing. There was nothing but a mountain of charred corpses and rubble.'

They found the corpse of Sakue's elder sister at her house. Her mother's body was lying next to that of a neighbour. Her brother, a medical student at Nagasaki University, came to look for his family. Though dazed, he seemed pleased that the girls had survived. But two days later he left, saying 'I don't want to die.' According to Sakue, he then grew 'as cold as ice'.

'The three of us who survived fled to the countryside with the help of some relations,' said Sakue. 'The bonds between our parents, brothers and sisters had been torn apart. Some barracks were constructed on the burnt-out fields of Nagasaki towards the end of 1945, and we started to live there together with our other surviving neighbours. It was an existence without electricity or food. Bleached skeletons were all that was left. A faint glow could be seen in the evenings – phosphorous emanating from the bones of the dead. Those who had managed to survive were unable to live or die in a humane manner, being forced to struggle with an utterly unknown disease.

'My younger sister tried her best, but defeated by poverty and disease, and longing for our mother, she finally ended her life by throwing herself under a train. I was irreconcilable as I cried out to her, tears running down my face, "Why did you have to die? Why couldn't you fight harder?"'

Eighteen-year-old Koichi Wada was luckier. His streetcar had been diverted to the terminal due to an accident. At 11.02am, the building was bathed by a blinding flash of light and struck by a violent explosion.

'The terminal was located three kilometers from the hypocenter, but I thought it had suffered a direct hit,' he said. 'I seemed to float up into the air before being thrown down onto the floor. Everything became dark and I felt something heavy on my back.

'After a while, the surroundings came gradually into view. I was shocked at the extent of the destruction. As my fellow workers pulled me out of the damaged building, I breathed a sigh of relief to find my arms and legs intact. The sounds of people crying out for help finally brought me back to my senses.'

From that point onward he devoted himself to rescue work. Every hospital and relief station in the city was jammed with seriously injured people and there were no medical supplies.

'All that could be done was to spread Mercurochrome or zinc ointment over the wounds and wrap them in gauze strips,' he said.

Yoshiro Yamawaki was 11 in 1945. On the morning of 9 August, his father had gone to work at Mitsubishi and his older brother, who was 14, was helping out in a weapons factory as part of a student mobilization. Yoshiro and his twin brother were at home because it was the summer holidays. Around 11am they were out on the veranda, then they got hungry and went into the sitting room at the back of the house.

'While we were sitting around the table a whitish-blue light shot across the room, then came a roar that seemed to shake the whole house,' said Yoshiro. 'The two of us got down on the tatami-mats and covered our eyes, ears and noses with our fingers, just like we had been taught to do. I thought that a bomb had directly hit our property, and that we would probably be buried alive there. After a few minutes the falling debris became more infrequent and while I lay there the voices of people in the neighbourhood screaming and crying reached my ears. Remaining on the ground, I lifted my head up and looked around to find everything completely changed.'

Yoshiro and his brother sought refuge in the tiny bomb shelter in their yard and waited for their father to come home. After an hour, his older brother turned up and took them to a larger bomb shelter dug into a cliffside. It was filled with crying children who had suffered burns to their exposed skin or were peppered with shards of glass and other fragments thrown by the blast.

The next morning, Yoshiro and his brothers set off to find their father.

'As we continued on, the damage grew worse and worse,'

said Yoshiro. 'The houses at the roadside had all burned to the ground and the trees and electric poles were scorched, although they remained standing. The factories on the other side of the river now looked like masses of crushed wire, with only the largest of their columns still standing.

'There were many dead bodies among the debris littering the roads. The faces, arms and legs had swollen up, making them look like black rubber dolls. When our shoes touched those bodies the skin would come peeling off just like that of an over-ripe peach, exposing the white fat underneath.'

There were dead bodies floating in the river as well. They were drawn to a corpse of a young woman of about 18 which seemed to have a long white cloth belt dragging behind. When they looked closer, they saw that the white belt was really her intestines, protruding from the side of her abdomen. There were so many corpses in the river that at one point they formed a human dam.

Arriving at their father's factory, they found it had been reduced to nothing but twisted metal and flame. They asked three men digging in the debris where their father was.

'Your father is over there,' said one of them, pointing to the ruins of an office building.

There they found their father's corpse, swollen and scorched just like all the others they had seen. Unable to take him home, they built a fire and burnt his body there. They went back to the ruins of their home to find a pot to put their father's remains in. By then, they were already inured to the sight of corpses and dismissed them merely as objects that blocked their way as they walked.

When they returned to their father's makeshift funeral pyre, they found that his body was only half burnt. They tried to collect his bones, but soon found the sight of their father's charred body unbearable so they decided just to take his skull and leave the rest of his body there. But when they touched their father's skull it crumbled and half-burned brains spilt out.

Over the years Yoshiro was admitted to Nagasaki Atomic Bomb Hospital 15 times for kidney and liver troubles and stomach cancer. Nevertheless, he was still alive at the age of 75.

The aftermath

At both Hiroshima and Nagasaki, many victims who survived the initial bombing died later of burns, radiation sickness, thyroid cancer and leukaemia. Survivors also suffered from cataracts. Men exhibited a catastrophically low sperm count. Women miscarried and there was a 27 per cent rate of premature births, compared to the normal rate of 6 per cent.

The question remained whether the dropping of the two atomic bombs was really necessary. The US Strategic Bombing Survey concluded that it was not. It said: 'Certainly prior to

The Enola Gay *lands at Tinian after dropping the first atomic bomb.*

31 December 1945 and in all probability prior to 1 November 1945, Japan would have surrendered even if the atomic bombs had not entered the war, even if Russia had not entered the war, and even if no invasion had been contemplated.'

However, it should also be remembered that on the days the atomic bombs were dropped, more Japanese died from conventional bombing and the naval bombardment inflicted on Japanese cities by the British and American ships that surrounded the islands.

Even after the atomic bomb had been dropped on Hiroshima, Japanese militarists were arguing that the US could not possibly have amassed enough radioactive material to continue such attacks. But after the bombing of Nagasaki, Emperor Hirohito – still a god in the eyes of the Japanese – told his government that 'to continue the war means nothing but the destruction of the whole nation'.

'The time has come,' he said, 'when we must endure the unendurable.'

The war is over

In the early hours of 10 August, a cable was sent to Japan's representatives in Stockholm and Berne accepting the Potsdam ultimatum, with the one proviso that the Japanese could keep their emperor. Truman held up any further attacks while the United States considered a response, finally taking a middle course and acknowledging the emperor by stating that his authority after the surrender would be exercised under the authority of the Supreme Commander of the Allied Powers. With British, Chinese, and Russian concurrence, the United States answered the Japanese on 11 August. Japan surrendered on 14 August 1945, ending the war.

Emperor Hirohito recorded a message to be broadcast at

noon on 15 August, calling for all Japanese to accept the surrender. The people of Japan had never heard his voice before. He warned them to 'beware of any outburst of emotion', as there were some who still wanted to fight to the finish.

Indeed there was a small group of officers in the palace itself who wanted to continue the war. On the night of 14 August, they approached General Nuzo Mori and asked him to join them. When he said that he would go and pray in the Meiji Shrine to help him make up his mind, they shot him, then used his seal in an attempt to locate the recording of the emperor's broadcast. When their coup failed, the officer who shot Mori committed *hara-kiri* on the Imperial Plaza. Other hard-liners also committed suicide.

'I might add,' said Admiral Soemu Toyoda, chief of the Naval General Staff and a member of the six-man Supreme War Guidance Council, 'that even on 15 August, when the Imperial decree to terminate the war was actually issued, we found it difficult to hold down the front-line forces who were all "raring to go", and it was difficult to hold them back.'

After the war, Major General Kiyoshi Miwa, vice-chief of staff to the Air Army, told his captors: 'As far as the army is concerned, the termination of the war was declared by the emperor and not by the army.'

On 30 August the first American occupation forces, accompanied by a small British contingent, arrived at Yokosuka. Then at 9am on 2 September the new Japanese foreign minister Mamoru Shigemitsu went on board the USS *Missouri* in Tokyo Bay. He signed the surrender document on behalf of the emperor and the Japanese government. This was accepted on behalf of the Allies by General Douglas MacArthur. Then a scratchy record of *The Star-Spangled Banner* was played over the ship's PA system and World War II was officially over.

Chapter Twelve
The Public Domain

The veil of secrecy that had hidden the atomic bomb project had been lifted on 6 August, with President Truman's announcement of the Hiroshima raid to the American people. The bombing of Nagasaki was also carried on the news. The Manhattan Project came into fuller view with the release of the Smyth Report on 12 August, which contained general technical information calculated to satisfy public curiosity without disclosing any atomic secrets. Americans were astounded to learn of the existence of the vast, nationwide, top-secret operation with its massive plants, payroll, and labour force comparable in size to the American automobile industry. Some 130,000 people were employed by the project at its peak, among them many of the nation's leading scientists and engineers.

From the time S-1 became public knowledge until the Atomic Energy Commission succeeded it on 1 January 1947, the Manhattan Engineer District continued to control the nation's nuclear programme. Groves remained in command, intent on protecting America's lead in nuclear weapons by completing and consolidating the organization he had presided over for three years in challenging wartime conditions.

According to a plan approved by Stimson and Marshall in late August 1945, Groves shut down the thermal diffusion plant in the K-25 area on 9 September and put the Alpha tracks at Y-12 on standby during September as well. The improved K-25 gaseous diffusion plant now provided feed directly to the Beta units. Hanford's three piles continued in operation, but one of the two chemical separation areas was closed.

Los Alamos was assigned the task of producing a stockpile of atomic weapons, although the actual weapon assembly was to be done at Sandia Base in Albuquerque, where engineering and technical personnel were relocated with the staff previously stationed at Wendover Field in western Utah.

Operation Crossroads

In July 1946, during Operation Crossroads, the Manhattan Project tested its third and fourth plutonium bombs. These

The 'Baker' explosion, part of the Operation Crossroads, a nuclear weapon test by the United States military at Bikini Atoll, Micronesia, on 25 July 1946.

tests were conducted in front of a large invited audience of journalists, scientists, military officers, congressmen and foreign observers at Bikini Atoll in the Pacific.

The third bomb, Shot Able, was dropped from a B-29 on 1 July. It sank three ships and performed as well as its two predecessors from a technical standpoint, though it failed to fulfil its pre-test publicity build-up. So two weeks later, Shot Baker was detonated from 90 feet under water on the morning of 15 July. Baker produced a spectacular display as it wreaked havoc on a 74-vessel fleet of empty ships and spewed thousands of tons of water into the air. Both Able and Baker yielded explosions equivalent to 21,000 tons of TNT, though Baker introduced a new, more subtle hazard of the atomic age – immediate, concentrated radiation fallout. Able and Baker were the final weapon tests conducted by the Manhattan Project and the last American tests until the Atomic Energy Commission's Sandstone series began in the spring of 1948.

The United States held a monopoly on atomic weapons during the 16 months of Groves's peacetime tenure, but less than three years after the Atomic Energy Commission succeeded the Manhattan Engineer District, the Soviet Union made its first successful test of an atomic bomb.

On 1 November 1952, the US tested its first hydrogen bomb, masterminded by Edward Teller. The USSR followed suit on 12 August 1953.

The ramifications of the Manhattan Project are with us to this day. During the Cold War, the Soviet Union and the US built up huge stockpiles of nuclear weapons that could destroy the world many times over. In the Cuban Missile Crisis of 1962, the world hovered on the brink of destruction and drew back.

Successive treaties contained the proliferation of nuclear weapons, banned tests and led to some disarmament. The fall of the Berlin Wall and the collapse of the Soviet Union in 1981 were heralded as the end of the Cold War, but relations

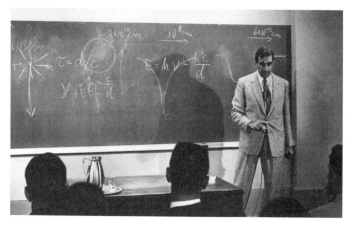

The legacy: Edward Teller left Los Alamos in 1946 and returned to the University of Chicago as a professor. He is seen here teaching a class at General Dynamics in the 1950s.

between the West and Russia have become frosty again, though there is no explicit nuclear confrontation.

However, hostile neighbours India and Pakistan have nuclear weapons. North Korea also has them and its 'Supreme Leader' Kim Jong-un frequently makes belligerent statements. Israel has never officially confirmed or denied having nuclear weapons, but it is suspected of having several hundred nuclear warheads. Consequently, Iran has expressed the desire to run a nuclear weapons programme in violation of the Nuclear Nonproliferation Treaty of 1968. But whatever the results of 21st-century tensions may be, it was the Manhattan Project that let the nuclear genie out of the bottle.

Index